ABOUT THE AUTHOR

Hans Verwer was born in Amsterdam, grew up in Bergen aan Zee, and attended the Latin school at Alkmaar. While still in school, she created dances and costumes for school performances. She was a pupil of Lily Green in Amsterdam and later went to Paris to study ballet with Lubov Egorova, former ballerina of the Imperial Russian Ballet. After her return to Holland, she married and taught ballet at Leiden.

Before the Second World War, Mrs. Verwer was, like so many others, strongly drawn to so-called Modern Dancing, and in later years her interest turned toward "abstract" creations of classical ballet and "ethnic" forms. After the war, she became a ballet critic —first of the *Haagsch Dagblad,* then of the monthly *Danskroniek,* of which she later became editor.

The author possesses an extensive archive of domestic (Dutch) and foreign dances, choreographers, ballets, and dancers.

ABOUT THE TRANSLATOR

Henry Mins received his M.A. and Ph.D. degrees from Columbia University and has been a consultant in Russian for the *Journal of Philosophy and Phenomenological Research* and a consultant for the *Little Golden Encyclopedia.* Although a writer in his own right (he has just completed a work on philosophy), Dr. Mins has founded a company that specializes in translations. He is a member of the Board of Directors of the American Translators Association.

SWAN LAKE
(Margot Fonteyn and Michael Somes)

Guide to the
BALLET

BY

HANS VERWER

Translated from the Dutch by Henry Mins

BARNES & NOBLE, INC.

PUBLISHERS • BOOKSELLERS • SINCE 1873

PREFACE

This book "describes" many works from ballet history. The quotation marks around "describes" serve only as a reminder that the most important element of a ballet—its essential characteristic, the dance itself—can not be described. The descriptions and discussions of periods and specific ballets are not ends in themselves; they do, however, serve to establish in advance our acquaintance with period, subject, and style and to lead us thereby to the essence of the art of ballet.

What is essential in ballet is the dance, not the subject or story. As an independent art the dance can exist without scenery, without costumes, without subject—although not without music. The movements usually vary with each ballet according to the dancer and the ballet company and comprise, within the framework of the choreographer's construction and the creative structure, the true dance art, which must be seen in order to be fully comprehended.

H. V.

TABLE OF CONTENTS

LIST OF ILLUSTRATIONS

Frontispiece: *Swan Lake* (Margot Fonteyn and Michael Somes)

The following illustrations appear between pages 104–5

1

The Origins of the Ballet

Many books point out that the dance is as old as mankind, and this statement can be accepted if we consider the concept of the dance in a very broad sense. We know little about the history of the dance in the centuries before the modern era, but we may be sure that it has always played an important role in the life of Western peoples. The art of the dance, however, involves much more than the mere physical activity of dancing. Moreover the *ballet*—by which we mean the dance form whose technique is based on the five positions introduced late in the seventeenth century by Charles Louis Beauchamps, dance master of Louis XIV—extends even beyond the art of the dance.

The origins of the dance may be traced to ancient times, as shown by extant paintings of Egyptian dances at religious rites and festivals. Various dance forms—war, ritual, and Dionysiac dances—were in use at the zenith of Greek civilization. Life-sized pictures from Tuscany attest to an Etruscan dance culture. Later, at the height of their power and influence, the Romans, who were officially, at least, less devoted than the Greeks had been to the dance, employed thousands of women dancers, many of whom earned fees equivalent to those earned by leading dancers today.

Dancing was popular among the peoples of western Europe during the early centuries of the Christian era. Although we do not know the music, the melodies, or the dance steps of the various countries, we do know the different types of musical instruments which were used: flutes of various kinds, stringed instruments, castanets, and, later on, bagpipes.

Dance customs of this early period persisted in the next— along with or as part of the ritual of the Church. In the Middle Ages men and women danced in the church squares, round about the church, and (in the miracle and mystery plays) even in the churches. But there is little that we can say definitely about the music or the dance steps that were used.

In the fifteenth century, Italy achieved its greatest cultural flowering, a fact not unrelated to the large increase in wealth of the upper classes. The nobility took pleasure in recreation, and many people who had readily accumulated wealth spent it freely for this purpose, sometimes in a deplorable manner. Religious feeling receded, and in its stead came an urge toward worldly beauty and joy in life, coupled with a kind of spiritual nihilism. Scholars and artists entered the service of the wealthy, pleasure-loving bourgeoisie. Renaissance culture was something confined to the elite, and, as in later centuries, the cultural and financial elite created the conditions for the development of the art of the dance. The slightest occasion was an excuse for a celebration; and if there was no occasion, one was made. No feast, festival, pageant, or staged celebration could be dreamed of without dancing, even in the dining hall of the pope; and no less a person than Leonardo da Vinci designed the decorations, stage machinery, and 287 elaborate costumes for a great feast in Mantua.

Then England, France, and Spain arrived on the scene. Although it was generally well known in these countries that the prosperity in Italy was accompanied by a dubious morality, nevertheless they took Italian culture as their model, and great festivities were thereafter features of French and Italian courts.

In 1533 Catherine de Médicis, the homely daughter of a

Florentine banker, was married to Henry II, the successor of Francis I to the throne of France. Catherine had a veritable passion for everything that was fine and splendid. The fact that she lived at a time when things were anything but easy for France did not matter to her; it seemed to be just one more reason for her to hold celebrations. Catherine obtained the assistance of an Italian named Baltazarini, known in France as Balthazar de Beaujoyeaulx, probably the first choreographer of whom we have any record. Festivities organized under his direction were notable for their allegorical figures, medieval surroundings and steps, bizarre costumes, and arrangements on a flat surface. We cannot hold it against Beaujoyeaulx that his ideas of dance form were limited, for the fashion prevailing in his time did not allow him many other possibilities. The extremely pompous costumes limited the movements of the body to stately strides.

The dance festivities sponsored by Catherine de Médicis were named "ballets comiques de la reine." The entertainment combined music, song, dance, processions, recitations, mechanical effects, and elaborate scenery. One of the best-known was *Circe*. This ballet was presented on October 15, 1581, to honor the betrothal of Catherine's sister Marguerite to the Duc de Joyeuse, and the production was quite long, lasting about five and one half hours. Beaujoyeaulx was acclaimed for his arrangements. Throughout Europe this form of entertainment was widely imitated; in France alone, eighty of these "ballets" were performed before 1610.

Toward the end of the sixteenth century two significant books by dance masters were published: *Il Ballarino* (1580) by Fabrito Caroso da Sermoneta, and *Orchésographie* (1588) by Thoinot Arbeau. These books described specific steps, simultaneously giving the sequence of actions on the dance floor; but neither author was concerned with spatial effects in the dance. In *Orchésographie* Arbeau also laid the foundation for the five basic positions of classic ballet that were formulated a hundred years later by Charles Beauchamps. Dance masters (later called *maîtres de ballet*) and choreographers (those who design and set the steps) have very different roles in the dance world, although these functions, as with Sermoneta and Arbeau, have sometimes been combined very well.

In France the tradition of festivities, established by Catherine, continued after her death. Writers who furnished the texts of the stories often inserted references, openly or by implication, to political matters, but the music must have been dull and monotonous. Courantes, pavanes, and gavottes were among the dances performed. Until 1630 only the nobles of the court danced. Beginning in that year, it became the custom to employ professional dancers, especially for the *divertissements* (entertainments consisting of a series of unrelated dances).

Court ballets and spectacles reached their fullest flowering during the reign of Louis XIV, who was an enthusiastic dancer and who received the name *Le Roi Soleil* from the part he played as Sun King in one of the ballets. He made his debut in *Cassandre* in 1651 and remained a devotee for nearly two decades, making his last appearance, in the ballet *Flora,* in 1669. The King was always the glorious center of attraction, frequently appearing as a Roman emperor with his nobles arrayed in order of rank around him. The costumes had become less ponderous and bulky, but headdresses still remained exaggerated.

Another type of spectacle presented during Louis XIV's reign was the *ballet à cheval* (ballet on horseback). One of these ballets was given in Paris in 1662 with 200 groups and 500 participants in very costly costumes. A *ballet à cheval* involving hundreds of participants was given in Vienna in 1667 to honor King Leopold I. The costumes were embroidered with silver thread and bedecked with jewels. Plumes as high as a man adorned the heads of the nobles. Even the horses wore jeweled ornaments. Some of the original sketches for these ballets have been preserved, and these show that all preparations were made with meticulous care. Compared to them the choreographic notations of modern choreographers look like children's drawings.

In 1661 a milestone in the history of ballet occurred when

Louis XIV established the Académie Royale de Danse. Louis appointed as directors of the new institution his dance master Charles Beauchamps and thirteen *maîtres de ballet,* who were charged with watching over the purity of the dance and with making the dance systematic. Beauchamps elaborated upon the principles of Arbeau, adding the movement of the leg from the hip and introducing the five positions. Technique now made rapid strides. The dance, no longer a hobby for amateurs, now became a profession. The special technique of the dance made it possible for choreographers to evolve; and we shall see that in the course of time choreographers and dancers cooperated to raise the technical standards of dance art.

Jean Baptiste Lully (1632–1687) became director of the Académie in 1672. He composed music, danced, and put ballets together. At this time the form of the ballet did not differ very much from the form of the opera. In the ballet, scenes were danced to words spoken or sung, and in the opera there was singing and from time to time dancing. But it was true even then that the ballet dancer had to be the master of a broader technique than the dancer at the opera.

In 1681 Lully collaborated with Beauchamps in the famous ballet *Le Triomphe de l'Amour* for the court at Versailles. Ladies of the court participated, and the great success of the work led to the decision to perform it in Paris as well. Since court ladies could not appear there, Lully, according to the convention of the day, should have filled these women's roles with men in masquerade. No one had ever objected to this kind of travesty (which shows that opinions and prejudices often depend on conventions and traditions). But Lully, after long consideration, decided to break with convention; he sought and finally found four beauties willing to appear on stage. Thereafter women were accepted as professional dancers; and Lully, probably inadvertently, thus placed a spoke in the wheel of ballet progress, for the result of having attractive women perform on stage was to distract attention from the creative element that makes the ballet worthy of being called an art. A beautiful figure on the stage is apt to monopolize the spectators' attention. In the preromantic period that follows we hear more about women dancers than about ballets and choreographers. The danseuse, as George Balanchine says, was to become the queen of the ballet. And yet it is always the choreographer who is the creator in the art of the dance; the male and female dancers are only executant artists.

The first favorite of the Paris public was La Camargo (1710–1770). A woman with magnificent legs, she shortened her skirts and mastered "elevation" (a certain lightness that gives the impression that the center of gravity is not on the ground but in the air). In addition she could easily execute an *entrechat quatre* (a leap from the fifth position, in which the feet interchange positions rapidly in the air) and a *petite batterie*.

Her rival was Marie Sallé (1707–1756). Sallé detested mannerisms and utilized her natural grace. Although less of a virtuoso than La Camargo, she had just as many admirers. Since she formed lasting friendships with men such as Voltaire and Garrick, she was probably a person of high intelligence. She wanted to reform the dance, and to this end she wore lighter garb, used no ornaments, and let her hair hang loose. Sallé is credited with having been the first of the great *terre à terre* dancers (i.e., one who can perform steps on the ground but who has poor elevation).

At about the same time, there was a male dancer, Gaetano Vestris, so expertly endowed that he became popularly known by the appropriate nickname *dieu de la danse* (god of the dance). Vestris (1729–1808), an Italian, was one of the first in a long line of important male dancers. He developed the technique of the leap and was also the first dancer to perform without a mask (in the revival of Noverre's *Médée et Jason*, 1770, when he was highly praised for the excellence of his mime). Subsequently Maximilien Gardel (1741–1787), another leading *danseur* of the day, discarded the mask in his performances at the Paris Opéra.

Jean Georges Noverre (1727–1810) was the first great theoretician in the art of ballet. Trained by Louis Dupré at the Paris Opéra, he had very advanced ideas about the dance, which he expressed in his famous *Lettres sur la Danse et sur les Ballets* (1760). One of his theses was that the dance must be (and is) able to express any emotions it needs without any support from song or the spoken word. He also wanted to reform costumes and to do away with masks.

Unable to put his ideas into effect in Paris, Noverre went to England to obtain training in pantomime from the actor David Garrick. Then he went to Stuttgart and eventually to Vienna, where he developed his *ballet d'action* and taught dancing to Marie Antoinette. Characters drawn from the list of Roman heroes were discarded, and shepherds and shepherdesses gradually replaced them. Finally, through the intervention of Marie Antoinette, then Queen of France, Noverre achieved his greatest desire: In 1776 he was appointed *maître de ballet* at the Paris Opéra.

The French Revolution made it impossible for Noverre to remain in France. He fled to England, where he lived in poverty, returning to France shortly before he died. Of his 150 ballets, we unfortunately know almost nothing. Noverre's influence, however, was to be felt in many countries during the nineteenth century. One of his main ideas—the feasibility of combining dance and pantomime—has been generally accepted throughout the ballet world by *maîtres de ballet*.

2

The Preromantic Ballet

The period of Noverre and his pupils—from 1750 to 1830—is usually referred to in history as Rococo, Louis Seize, Directoire, Empire, and Biedermeier; in ballet history we call this era "preromantic."

Noverre had not only many disciples but also many imitators. As interest in the art of the dance grew everywhere in Europe, his followers spread far and wide. Charles le Picq (1749–1806), one of Noverre's favorite pupils, was ballet master at St. Petersburg, where Tsar Peter the Great had founded a ballet in 1703. Charles Didelot (1767–1837), who succeeded him, created over fifty ballets and effected many changes in the teaching of ballet. Vincenzo Galeotti (1733–1816), an Italian, spent many years with the Copenhagen Royal Ballet, which he first joined in 1775. And Salvatore Viganò (1769–1821), who made a significant contribution as ballet master of La Scala, Milan, probably received his training from Jean Dauberval (1742–1806), a pupil and follower of Noverre.

Forebodings of revolution began to appear in France, for the people were sated with the absolute monarchy. There was a striving toward simple and rural things, a back-to-nature movement advocated by Jean Jacques Rousseau. The ruling class settled down outside of Paris and, not satisfied with a single Versailles, built innumerable luxurious châteaux. At Petit Trianon, Marie Antoinette and ladies of her court showed their admiration for peasant life. At Rambouillet there was a magnificent barn, where the Queen and her friends could put on shows with real cattle. Country life became idealized. The nobility freed itself from the strict classical ideas of the Renaissance; ornament became the accepted art form. But the game of playing shepherds and shepherdesses so charmingly portrayed by Watteau, Boucher, and Fragonard was a farce; these shepherds and shepherdesses never tended a herd. In ballet the result was the introduction of the *pas de deux*, the first typically erotic form in the ballet. The gods were replaced by rustic characters. Noverre himself was at his best with Mozart's *Les Petits Riens*, danced by the eighteen-year-old Auguste Vestris, who leaped so prettily and had a new way of gliding.

Two ballet works from this period have come down to us: Vincenzo Galeotti's *Les Caprices de Cupidon et du Maître de Ballet* and Dauberval's *La Fille Mal Gardée*, both from 1786. The first work, contrary to most ballets of the period, includes a deity among its characters, albeit one generally associated with eroticism. The second ballet presents a love idyll in the country. This was understandable, since the heroic pantomime had disappeared from the stage by 1760. Choreographers turned toward the folk dance, and found there an inexhaustible source of inspiration for the stage.

In those days it was not the choreographers but the dancers who reigned supreme. Thus Madeleine Guimard (1743–1816), a *demi-caractère* dancer, half noble and half comic, was the idol of the public. She had more grace than skill, appeared in simple costumes, and performed brilliantly in shepherdess roles. It is said that in her private life she constantly sought the love she depicted on the stage. Ballets, reportedly of a scandalous nature, were occasionally given in her home.

Male dancers were still important in the ballet. Vestris came to Paris from Italy. Later he worked with Noverre in Germany.

He had a reputation as a mimic dancer with a sure elegance. His mistress Marie Allard was the mother of his son Auguste Vestris (1760–1842), who achieved fame for his skill as a dancer and notoriety for his bad manners. Reports of his skill indicate that the young man's elevation must have been extraordinary, his *entrechats* and pirouettes brilliant. Auguste gave lessons to Fanny Elssler, Didelot, and Jules Perrot. In addition, the Paris Opéra had the Gardel brothers. Maximilien Gardel was the son of a ballet master of the King of Poland. It is said that he and Auguste Vestris collaborated in inventing the *rond de jambe*. It was Gardel who took his mask off to show the spectators that he had been playing the role assigned to Vestris on a certain evening. Besides working as a dancer at the Paris Opéra he was a choreographer; he danced with Guimard in the performance of some of his works. His brother, Pierre Gardel (1785–1840) was far less prominent even though he was for a long time *maître de ballet* and composed several complete ballets.

Little need be said about the standard of choreography then prevailing. We can safely assume that it was not high, for evidence suggests that the choreographers depended mainly on sentimental waltzes and thin romantic plots.

The outbreak of the French Revolution dealt a severe blow to the art of the ballet. Noverre, as mentioned above, went to England, and Pierre Gardel just managed to keep his head above water. Even the aid of Robespierre and of the noted painter Jacques Louis David (a sponsor of Guimard) failed to preserve this idyllic era of the ballet. When Napoleon permanently put an end to the game of shepherd and shepherdess, the ballet reverted to the moods and motifs of earlier days. For a time classicism reigned supreme again. Costumes became even simpler. Satin shoes were replaced by something that looked more like a sandal. Geometric figures came back into choreography, but less rigidly than during the Baroque era; and the diagonal was reintroduced. Movements became more stylized. The costume designer Maillot made what was probably the most important contribution of this period: the close-fitting tights that are still called the dancer's *maillot*.

In 1812 the focus of ballet shifted to Italy where Salvatore Viganò was appointed *maître de ballet* at La Scala, Milan. The Italians are still proud of this master, who was very musical and who was apparently the first to create what were called sym-- phonic ballets. The element of pantomime became less important. Viganò set dances to the music of Rossini, Beethoven, and Mozart; he devoted special attention to the *corps de ballet* without neglecting the soloist. Nevertheless, although Viganò must have been an outstanding choreographer, contributing much to the art of ballet, none of the forty or more ballets he created has remained in the repertoire. In 1837 he was succeeded by Carlo Blasis (1797–1878).

In Russia, foreign ballet masters, chiefly Italian, were used exclusively in St. Petersburg. Jean Baptiste Landé came there in 1734, and at his request the Academy of Dancing was established in 1738. Afterward others arrived: among them Hilferding, Angiolini, Granger and then, in 1786, Charles le Picq. The art of ballet in Russia experienced its first great changes with Charles Didelot. When he came to St. Petersburg in 1801, he introduced the *maillot* and the glide. The latter, however, was not the glide of Auguste Vestris; this one was done with the aid of ropes, and thus people began to speak of "Didelot's flying ballets," wherein he would have as many as fifty dancers representing doves. There is something more that can be said to his credit: his opposition to the "star system." Didelot's contribution to the development of the Russian ballet at the time must be described as monumental.

The preromantic period, as a whole, can be regarded as an era in which outstanding personal contributions were made by individual dancers and dance masters. Nevertheless, so far as the real art of the ballet is concerned, little more was achieved than the introduction of the *pas de deux* and certain technical possibilities for dancers.

BALLETS

Les Caprices de Cupidon et du Maître de Ballet ("The Whims of Cupid and the Ballet Master")

Ballet in one act. Choreography: Vincenzo Galeotti (real name: Tomazelli). Music: Jens Lolle. Première: October 31, 1786, at the Royal Theater, Copenhagen.

CHARACTERS: Cupid; Tyrolean couple; Quaker couple; Greek couple; Norwegian couple; old couple; French couple; Danish couple; three Negro couples; four priests or pages.

❧

Cupid is seated in the center of the stage. Pages lead in the various couples in the order given above. Once on stage, a couple executes a folk dance. When the dance is over, the pages lead the couple out and return with the next pair. After all the couples have appeared before Cupid, they come back to ask for permission to marry. The boys and men stand on the right, the girls and women on the left. Cupid indicates that he consents to the choices of their hearts. All are blindfolded and Cupid is to join their hands. But Cupid seems to have an idea: He amuses himself by changing the partners. After the blindfolds have been removed, the men and women discover some unusual unions—for instance, the Norwegian woman has been linked by Cupid with a Negro; the Quaker lady with the Norwegian; one of the Negro women with the Greek.

There is great confusion. Everyone tries to get rid of the partner Cupid has assigned him; Cupid looks on, laughing. The curtain falls, without any solution being given.

❧

This comic ballet by Galeotti is the only one of his approximately fifty ballets that has remained in repertory up to the present. It was performed almost continuously during Galeotti's lifetime and throughout the active career of Auguste Bournonville (1805–1879), Galeotti's pupil and successor at the Royal Danish Ballet. Harald Lander (1905–   ), present ballet master of the Royal Danish Ballet, combined oral tradition and the findings of research in Danish archives to reconstruct the ballet for the Paris Opéra (première February 27, 1952) in an extravagant but charming setting by Chapelain-Midy. Little has been changed in this ballet since 1786, probably because the work consists of not much more than a series of well-known folk dances.

In 1786 dancers did not yet perform on *pointe* but on *demi-pointe* (half-toe), and Galeotti, as a contemporary of Noverre, emphasized pantomime. Thus, this amusing and charming ballet has always seemed just right for young people not yet capable of dancing on *pointe*. Hans Brenaa once staged a modified version of this ballet in Denmark, with Cupid dancing on *pointe*.

All in all, Galeotti's ballets have had more than 2,250 performances.

La Fille Mal Gardée ("Vain Precautions")

Ballet in two acts, three scenes. Book and Choreography: Jean Dauberval. Music: various composers (see note following description of the ballet). Première: date and place unknown (Cyril Beaumont believes that the première took place in London in 1786).

CHARACTERS: Simone, a rich farm woman (traditionally played by a man); her daughter, Lise; Colas (sometimes called Colin), Lise's beloved; Thomas, a winegrower; his son, Alain; villagers; harvest workers.

❧

ACT I, SCENE 1. A village. Left front, the house of Simone. Opposite, the dairy. Daybreak.

As the curtain goes up, a number of farm workers are going into the fields. Lise comes out of her home and is disappointed that her beloved Colas is not among the workers. She goes to her dairy and emerges with a bowl of milk, which she places on the ground. In order to show Colas that she did not forget their rendezvous, she takes off a ribbon and hangs it on a tree.

Hardly has she gone back into the farmhouse when Colas appears. He sends away the friends who are with him and runs on tiptoe to the window of the farmhouse hoping to see Lise. Disappointed that he does not hear or see anything, he is about to leave when he discovers the ribbon on the tree. Delighted and surprised, he takes the ribbon and ties it to his stick. He kisses the ribbon and blows a kiss to the window where he hopes Lise might be. While he is doing this, he is caught by Mother Simone, who is not pleased to have this farm hand as her daughter's suitor. In rage, she shakes her fist at him and throws first her cap, then a basket, at his head. Colas dodges the basket and takes to his heels. Lise, who has just come out of the house, picks up the cap and the basket and hands them to her mother. Simone scolds her daughter, who tries to defend herself. Simone will not listen to her.

A number of villagers come in and ask for work on the harvest. Simone hires them, and Lise begins to prepare their meal, which will be eaten in the fields. Simone gives each of the workers a sickle. Lise finishes preparing the meal and asks to go into the fields with the farm hands. Simone holds her back because she knows Lise would meet Colas, and that is something Simone would like to prevent.

Colas, at a distance, comes to see whether Lise will manage to get away to the fields. Lise indicates that she has to stay at the house. She tries once more to persuade her mother to let her go, but Simone refuses and orders her daughter to churn some butter.

Simone goes out to get the churn, and Colas, taking advantage of her momentary absence, hides nearby. Simone returns with the churn and leaves again; Colas emerges. Longingly he holds his hands out to Lise, but she hesitates to put hers in his. As Colas, in disappointment, turns to leave she reaches for the ribbon on his staff. She takes it and puts it into her bodice. Colas, rejoicing over this gesture, thinks that he might steal a kiss. Lise bashfully refuses, pointing out that she has to churn the butter. Colas offers to help her. Not much work is done, however, because they are excited at being together. Footsteps are heard, and Colas hides again. Lise churns vigorously. Some girls enter and ask Lise whether she is going with them into the fields. Simone, ever watchful, comes in and sends the girls away. Then she looks at Lise's work and observes that she has not done much. Lise receives another reprimand.

Now the winegrower Thomas appears with his son Alain. Simone, the shrewd mother, immediately suspects that Thomas has come to ask for Lise's hand in marriage to his son. Simone promptly consents. At that moment Lise arrives and tries in vain to find out why the three of them are so happy. Simone gives Lise permission to go out into the fields. Alain offers Lise his arm, but Lise declines and takes Thomas' arm. Simone, holding onto Alain's arm, follows the pair.

ACT I, SCENE 2. A large field with a number of farm workers. Noon.

Colas announces that it is time to eat. Simone, Lise, Thomas, and Alain go to the cottage, and Colas greets his neighbors. Alain sits down near the girls, but Colas shows him to a seat next to his father. After the meal there is a dance. Colas tries again to sit next to Lise but is detected by the ever-watchful Mother Simone. Thomas and Alain do not like the way things are going; they become jealous and depart. One of the young men jokes with the girls. He plays a dance tune on a flute. The girls tease him and snatch his flute. The owner chases them. The fun is disturbed by a sudden thunderclap. A violent squall drives everyone to shelter. Colas of course is close to Lise, but Simone is still present to prevent their being alone.

ACT II. Interior of Mother Simone's farmhouse. To the right, a door. At the left, a staircase leading to an upstairs room.

Simone and Lise come in, each with a sheaf of wheat. Mother Simone is worn out and drops into the nearest chair. She suggests that they do some spinning and Lise quickly gets things ready. Simone meanwhile shuts the door that Lise has left ajar. Lise enters with the spinning wheel and two distaffs. The women begin spinning, but Simone, overcome with weariness, soon drops off to sleep. Lise believes she can take the door key from her mother, but her plan is thwarted as Simone wakes from her light slumber. She now suggests that her daughter dance, while she accompanies her on the tambourine. As Lise dances, Simone dozes off again. Lise has noticed that Colas is nearby, but when she tries to go to him, Simone wakes up and beats on the tambourine. Lise continues to dance, and Colas leaves. Mother and daughter together execute a dance, which is interrupted by the farm hands who knock on the door. They bring in the sheaves, and Simone pays them their wages. The workers indicate that they would not mind a drink. Simone goes down to the cellar with them, but not until she has carefully locked Lise in the room. Lise looks sadly out the window, then leaves the window and walks aimlessly along the sheaves. Suddenly she cries out, for Colas is there: He has been hiding behind the sheaves. Lise bids him not to come a step closer. It is difficult for both of them to restrain their affection. Lise resumes her spinning but in a moment bursts into tears and drops the distaff. Colas thinks she has fainted and rushes to her; he tries to dry her tears with his handkerchief. Lise gives him her handkerchief, and both are deeply moved.

Footsteps are heard, and Colas escapes up the stairs to Lise's room, just in time. Mother Simone does not notice the escape, but she does see the handkerchief in Lise's hand and asks her daughter how she got it. Lise answers that it is Simone's. Simone is not at all sure; she suspects that while she was away Lise must have talked with Colas through the window. She sends her daughter upstairs, not realizing that she is sending Lise right into Colas' arms. Thomas arrives to tell Simone he has made all the arrangements for the marriage. Alain and the notary are with him. Alain calls the villagers in to tell them of his good fortune, and Simone then allows him to go upstairs for his bride. As soon as Alain puts his foot on the first step, Colas appears at the head of the stairs to bar his way. Simone is terrified. Colas and Lise beg Simone's permission to let them get married. The villagers support Lise and Colas. The mayor, too, says that Simone should give her consent, which she finally does. Thomas and Alain are crushed.

A general festival follows.

Information about this ballet has been derived from data of the first Danish production in 1786. The work was performed in Bordeaux, France, in 1789 under the title *Le Ballet de la Paille, ou il n'est qu'un pas du mal au bien* ("The Straw Ballet or it is only a step from evil to good"). Here it was given a political coloring, which was then quickly deleted. The music was apparently put together hurriedly, for the original accompaniment consisted of a series of folk tunes. When the ballet came into repertory at the Paris Opéra in 1827, music by Louis Joseph Ferdinand Hérold was used. Later Paul Taglioni chose music by Johann Wilhelm Hertel for the Berlin production. At St. Petersburg a medley was prepared from compositions by Delibes, Drigo, Hertel, Minkus, Pugni, Rubinstein, and others, and the choreography was attributed to Petipa and Ivanov. The work has been almost continually in repertory in Russia since the first Maryinsky presentation in 1885.

Because *Le Fille Mal Gardée* is a pantomime ballet best suited for ensembles that make the most of their soloists, it gives promising performers a chance to show their ability to mime and their technical prowess. The role of Mother Simone was originally (and still usually is) danced by a man. In the production presented by Anna Pavlova in London, the roles of Lise, Colas, and Mother Simone were danced, respectively, by Pavlova, Laurent Novikov, and Enrico Cecchetti. On November 12, 1938, the Mordkin Ballet staged Mordkin's revival of the work at the Alvin Theatre, New York. At that time the principal parts were taken by Lucia Chase, Mikhail Mordkin, and Dimitri Romanoff. Less than two years later, on January 19, 1940, Ballet Theatre presented Bronislava Nijinska's arrangement of the ballet at the Center Theater, New York, with Patricia Bowman, Yurek Shabelevsky, and Edward Caton. Frederick Ashton prepared an entirely new production for the Royal Ballet on January 28, 1960, with Nadia Nerina, David Blair, and Leslie Edwards; scenery and costumes were by Osbert Lancaster.

3

The Romantic Ballet

A new period of expansion in ballet came with the spread of Romanticism around 1830. In a sense it was a further development of the same trend during the preromantic period and of the promise held out by Noverre and his followers.

The heroic realism of the French Revolution had interrupted the course of the preromantic era. Under Napoleon, the "heroic" soon degenerated into a spurious patriotism dressed in pseudo-classic clothing. (After Napoleon's downfall, however, the old reactionary powers were reinstated in Europe, while simultaneously there was a rush toward industrialization. The individual was in danger of becoming a mere cog in a machine, and he felt the need of spiritual freedom. If he could not attain this goal, he reacted by taking refuge in dreams, in romanticism—a flight from reality which signified a discovery and recognition of the inner life of feelings, desires, and strong passions. In music, literature, and the ballet this inner life was evoked in the form of fairy tales and exotic fantasies.)

Indeed, it has been said that drastic changes in social relationships were the fundamental cause of the rise of Romanticism. The craftsman in the Middle Ages had been master of his own means of production; he owned his tools, workshop, and raw materials. As modern capitalism began to develop, the worker often became an employee laboring for and under the direction of the minority—the capitalists who owned the means of production. The producer or creator thus became separated from responsibility for the tools and final product. The consequent loss of his feeling of creativeness caused him to turn away from social reality and to take refuge within himself—in his imagination, dreams, and art. Thus the development of Romanticism is attributed to some extent to the early stages of capitalism which inaugurated a revolution in social relationships.

In the Romantic period—the age of Byron, Shelley, Keats, Stendhal, Heine, Liszt, Chopin, Schumann, and Wagner—the ballet went through a phase of enormous growth and flowering with respect to both technique and public interest. In technique the use of the *pointe* multiplied the possibilities of the dance, and the development of mimic art and pantomime furthered its expression. The ballet master directed his effort above all to the manifestation of human feelings and emotions.

In Denmark Antoine Bournonville followed in Galeotti's footsteps, and an Académie de Ballet was founded in 1829, where Bournonville and later his son Auguste (1805–1879) were ballet masters. Auguste studied with his father, with Galeotti, and with Vestris and became the leading ballet notable of his day; in fact, for decades he dominated the ballet school and the theater. We are indebted to him for his fine technique and for no less than fifty-three ballets, some of which are still in the Danish repertory.

In France the new movement began with Pierre Gardel, who had survived both the Revolution and Napoleon. Louis Milon (1765–1849) was his assistant. Nevertheless, until the 1840's the art of ballet in France made little progress. An era of real achievement followed thereafter, however, with outstanding contributions by Jean Coralli (1779–1854) and Jules Perrot (1810–1892), each of whom was both a *maître de ballet* and a choreographer.

In Italy, Carlo Blasis, whose *Treatise on the Dance* appeared in 1820, was *maître de ballet* in Milan after 1837 and was highly esteemed as a teacher.

In Russia, a ballet school was established in Moscow in 1807 and was directed by students of Didelot. Adam Glouchkovsky was the dominant figure from 1811 to 1840. In 1861 Carlo Blasis was called in, and he directed the work there until 1864.

England, Austria, and Germany also had ballet groups, but these depended chiefly on the work of foreign guest dancers, and no national ballet art was developed.

It was during the Romantic period that men developed a new attitude toward women, whose principal attractions and feminine charms were now magnified, as if men had suddenly found a fresh source of admiration and self-realization. From the early stages of Romanticism down to the present, the symbolic value of woman has become increasingly important for man; and this overvaluation of woman has been characteristic of ballet.

The new attitude of men toward women is reflected in the ballets by the overwhelmingly predominant position of the female dancer and the inane scraping together of fairy-tale material. Insofar as the problems of life are depicted, they appear in the oversimplified contacts between good and bad people, innocent girls and evil seducers, practical and idealistic individuals. The stories above all feature moonlight and mysterious forests inhabited by mysterious beings. The heroes have been replaced by specters—specters in tulle clothing, spirits of feminine beauty, the adored ballerinas. We may say that the romantic ballet was an escape from social reality into the charm and beauty (and sometimes the perfidy) of woman; and we may note that the effort was made to discover "woman," that is, her true nature—an effort which at first produced little more than an inventory of woman's erotic attractions.

The public wanted ballerinas to admire and worship, and the male dancers were pushed into the background as the choreographers highlighted the beauty and competitive chorus of the female dancers. Not much attention was given to the work of the choreographers. Ballerinas such as Marie Taglioni (1804–1884), Fanny Elssler (1810–1884), Fanny Cerito (1821–1899), Carlotta Grisi (1821–1899), and Lucile Grahn (1821–1907)—and not choreographers such as Jean Coralli (1779–1854), Jules Perrot (1810–1892), and Arthur Saint-Léon (1821–1870)—were borne aloft in triumph. Marie Taglioni, trained by her father, Filippo, took Paris by storm in *La Sylphide*. It is said that Taglioni invented dancing on *pointes*. She had excellent elevation, giving the impression of floating on air. Who was better qualified than she to portray an unearthly being? Her rival Fanny Elssler, from Vienna, was also trained for the ballet by Filippo Taglioni. England swore by Taglioni; but Elssler was the favorite of Paris. Elssler was more earthly, voluptuous, and beautiful, and she was famous for her character dances, particularly those of Russian, Spanish, Hungarian, and Polish origin. When she tried to play *La Sylphide,* however, she fell with a heavy thud. Only Théophile Gautier, French poet and critic, found a kind word to say about her performance. Elssler danced not only in Europe but also in America, where she found many devotees. Lucile Grahn of Copenhagen, considered the best technician, competed against Taglioni in *La Sylphide,* appeared in the celebrated *Pas de Quatre* in London, and won many admirers in Russia. In Milan, Perrot discovered Carlotta Grisi, who became famous for her creation of the role of Giselle in the ballet by that name. The Italian Fanny Cerito also became a very popular dancer. She danced in Naples, London, Vienna, and Paris. One of the quartet in the *Pas de Quatre,* she was widely acclaimed for her work in *Ondine* (1843), *La Vivandière* (1844), and *La Fille de Marbre* (1847).

Our primary source materials for this era—reports of critics—are filled with detailed descriptions of the charms of the lady dancers; and we also have lithographs of the lovely ballerinas and scandalous stories of their love affairs. These ballerinas, however, could not have achieved such fame if it had not been for the choreographers who provided them with the proper framework. How ironic that so many know the names of the popular dancers of the day, but so few the names of the great choreographers! Despite the excessive attention to ballerinas, a few ballets from this period have remained in repertory or have been successfully reconstructed.

About the middle of the century, interest in the ballerinas declined. In fact, after 1850 the heyday both of the ballerina and of the ballet itself was over in western Europe.

BALLETS

The Prisoner of the Caucasus*

Ballet in four acts. Book: Charles Didelot, after a story by Pushkin set in the reign of Tsar Alexander I (1801–1825). Choreography: Charles Didelot. Music: Cavos. Première: January 27, 1823, at the Bolshoi Theater in St. Petersburg.

CHARACTERS: Rostislav; his betrothed; his father; Kzelkia; the leader of the Tartars; Circassians, a people of the Western Caucasus; Russians.

ACT I. A camp of Tartars and Circassians near a river in the Caucasus.

The Tartars and Circassians, who have united to fight the Russians, amuse themselves in their camp by playing, dancing, and feasting. They sharpen their knives on the rocks. Women are busy with children. A child sleeping in a blanket hangs from a sword driven into a tree.

Suddenly there is a shriek from one of the women. An eagle has stolen the child. Pursued by the soldiers, the frightened bird drops the child, who is brought back safely.

Wild music announces the coming of a troupe of Circassians. They bring a captured Russian with them. Kzelkia, a Circassian girl, entreats the leader to pardon Rostislav, the prisoner. But all Rostislav wants is a weapon with which to defend himself. He is given the weapon and proves his ability; the leader is greatly

* See page 122 for contemporary version.

pleased and promises that his life will be spared. Kzelkia expresses admiration for the captured officer.

A sentry comes to announce that the Russians are approaching. They are looking for the captured officer. Preparations are made for battle, and the Circassians go out to fight the Russians. Kzelkia and Rostislav are left alone. When Kzelkia tells him that she has fallen in love with him, Rostislav asks her to desist and to leave him alone. She goes off sadly, but the prisoner calls her back. She throws herself into his arms, hopefully. He, however, shows her his engagement ring, and Kzelkia sinks to the ground distraught. She rises when she hears the sound of the returning Circassians, who bring with them a new captive whom Rostislav recognizes as his betrothed. Kzelkia reaches for her dagger to kill her rival, but humanity overcomes her desire for vengeance; she throws the deadly weapon away. She asks her leader to entrust the new prisoner to her care. Night falls. The warriors sleep. Kzelkia is alone with the two prisoners.

ACT II. The camp. Nighttime.

Kzelkia enters a tent with a file and other tools to liberate the captives. A fit of jealousy seizes her; nevertheless, she files through the prisoners' chains. When the two have been freed, they flee toward the river. Kzelkia faints. When she regains consciousness, she sees Rostislav's clothing and hurries to the river. A thunderstorm comes up. In the flashes of lightning the two fugitives can be seen swimming toward the far bank.

Rostislav's father arrives with Russian troops. He finds his son's clothes and, wild with rage, orders an attack on the sleeping camp, which is then devastated. The leader is taken prisoner and the Russians return to their territory, with torches blazing. Only Rostislav's father stays behind, mourning his son.

ACT III. The other side of the river. In the distance, the devastated village.

Rostislav's betrothed runs along the river bank. She has lost sight of her lover in the river and fears that he is dead. Overcome with fatigue and grief she sinks down and dies.

The storm subsides and now Kzelkia and Rostislav appear. They find the dead girl and kneel beside her body. The ghost of the girl appears and tells Rostislav to give her ring to the Circassian maiden. Rostislav tries to put his arms around the ghost, but it flees.

Rostislav's father approaches with his troops. The ghost returns, urges Rostislav's father to consent to the marriage of his son with the Circassian girl, and then vanishes again.

ACT IV. The palace of Rostislav's father.

The victory is celebrated with a festival in which Circassians and Tartars also take part. The father announces the marriage of his son Rostislav to the Circassian maiden. The Circassians and Tartars join the Russians.

⚭

Didelot did not follow Pushkin's story very closely. He added a second heroine to it: Rostislav's fiancée. The ending, in which the Circassians and the Tartars are merged with the Russian people, was probably dictated by suggestions from higher-up. As is well-known, the Russians fought for many years to subjugate these freedom-loving peoples, and the ending may therefore be thought of as a wish to be fulfilled later on. Didelot, who introduced the so-called flying ballets, made use of all his technical resources in this work, including the eagle's theft of the child and the appearance of the ghost. Pushkin was most considerate of Didelot and even told him that a French choreographer was worth more than all the Russian poets put together—and this while Didelot was butchering Pushkin's work.

Adam Glouchkovsky, Didelot's pupil and favorite, mounted the work again in 1827, with his wife Tatiana in the role of the Circassian maiden. Some sources attribute the entire work to Glouchkovsky, but it does not appear that he made many changes in the treatment.

La Sylphide

Ballet in two acts. Book: Adolphe Norruit (after Nodier). Choreography: Filippo Taglioni. Music: Jean Schneitzhoeffer. Scenery: Ciceri. Costumes: Eugène Lami. Première: March 12, 1832, at the Opéra, Paris.

CHARACTERS: the sylphid (spirit of the air, or young sylph); James, a Scotch farm boy; Gurn, a rival of James; Anna Reuben, James's mother; Effie; Magde; witches; sylphs; villagers.

ᕓᕓ

Act I. A farm in Scotland at daybreak. In the center, rear, a large window; left, a staircase leading to the upper story.

Gurn lies sleeping in a corner, dreaming of his beloved Effie, who is to marry James that day. James sits on a chair near him and dreams also. A sylphid kneels beside him, then flies over his head, and finally wakens him with a kiss on the forehead. He seeks his dream figure but it flies away through the chimney. Is he awake or dreaming? To solve the riddle, he wakes Gurn.

There is a knock at the door; Mother Reuben and Effie enter. Gurn offers Effie feathers from a bird he has caught. She thanks him in an offhand way and goes over to James, who is sitting strangely forlorn on this important day. Absently he kisses Effie's hand. Gurn wants to kiss Effie's hand too, but is repulsed. Ruefully he watches Mother Reuben give her consent to the marriage.

Effie's friends come in with their gifts. James pays little attention to all this. He is interested only in the chimney through which his dream figure flew. But what does he see there now? An ugly old woman named Magde, who is said to have magical powers. He tries to go to her, but Effie asks Magde to read her hand and tell her whether or not James loves her. There is consternation when the old woman declares that James does not love her. Gurn then asks her to read his hand. The old woman does so and replies, "Gurn really loves Effie." James is furious and drives the sorceress away; Effie says she does not believe any of it. The preparations for the wedding begin. Mother Reuben and Effie go upstairs; the girls follow.

James is left alone, torn in thought between Effie and his vision. Suddenly the window opens and the sylphid appears. She tells James how much she loves him and how she guards him against evil at night. James is moved and tells her about Effie, his bethrothed. The sylphid sorrowfully bids him farewell. Now she wants to die. James calls her back and says he will always be with her in his thoughts. The sylphid flies about joyfully and urges James to go with her. He hesitates. The sylphid kneels at his feet, and James, his passions again aroused, takes her in his arms and kisses her. Gurn, who has seen all this, hurries to tell Effie. James hears someone approach and quickly hides the sylphid under a woolen shawl on the armchair.

Girls enter laughing. In a festival which follows, the young people dance, while the older people drink. James's thoughts are still on the events of his dream, and he forgets to invite his bride to dance. Effie, however, leads him to the floor. The sylphid appears and mingles with the dancers, but she is visible only to James. He tries to embrace her, and the people think he has lost his mind. Finally it is time for the marriage ceremony. The marriage veil is placed on Effie's head and the ring is handed to her. When James takes his own ring from his finger as if to give the ring to Effie, the sylphid suddenly appears and snatches it from him, swearing that she will die if James marries Effie. James promptly resolves to follow the sylphid and both disappear behind the circle of friends. Effie is ready for the wedding ceremony, but when James is called there is no answer. Gurn announces that he has just seen the bridegroom and a young woman go off together into the hills. Effie is desolate, Mother Reuben is angry, and all are indignant. Gurn again declares his love to Effie, who is too overcome to answer. Mother Reuben thereupon takes her into her arms, while Gurn kneels down at Effie's feet.

ACT II. A forest with a large tree in the foreground. To the left, a rock with a cave. A dense mist everywhere. Nighttime.

Old Magde is immersed in her magic rites. She draws a circle three times around a great pot and then touches it with a large spoon. Witches come running and begin to dance around the pot, which begins to boil. A magic shawl adorned with jewels is then taken from the pot. The witches return to the cave.

The rising sun dispels the mist, and the forest can be seen more easily. James appears alone; in his hand is a bird's nest which he intends to offer the sylphid. Suddenly the sylphid appears and asks him what he has. When she sees it is a nest, she takes it from him and puts it in the treetop. She takes James by the hand and walks happily through the woods with him. At her call, her sister sylphs appear and gather round the pair. A game of hide-and-seek begins in which James tries but fails to catch his own sylphid. He gives up the chase in exhaustion and lies down on the ground, only to find his sylphid once more beside him. One by one the sylphs vanish, and James is left alone.

Effie returns to James's thoughts; he is disturbed for fear he may have chosen a dream figure instead of reality. He can not endure it that his sylphid constantly runs away; he wants his beloved to be always near him. Old Magde appears and asks whether she can help him. James gratefully accepts her offer, and the old witch gives him the magic shawl. When he turns around, the sylphid is with him again. James thinks that now is the time to test the shawl's magic powers. He puts the shawl on the sylphid's shoulders. Instantly her wings fall from her shoulders; she can fly no more. She puts her hands to her heart as if in mortal pain. James tries to take her in his arms, but she falls to the ground at his feet. Mocking laughter is heard from the cave. The sylphs descend from the trees to attend their young sister's last breath. James kneels beside her in despair.* The sylphs take the sylphid in their arms and carry her to the treetops.

Silence, broken only by the sound of a bagpipe and bells, returns to the forest. Through the trees a wedding procession can be seen: Gurn is leading Effie to the altar.

The romantic ballet really began with *La Sylphide,* which set the pattern for many later works. Its genesis goes back to Charles Nodier who, during his travels through Scotland, came under the influence of that romantic country and wrote the well-known story *Trilby.* Nourrit, a tenor at the Paris Opéra, prepared a synopsis based on this work and presented it to L. Véron, director of the Opéra, who assigned it to Taglioni. Schneitzhoeffer composed the music, and after a while the work was produced as a ballet. Lami designed an entirely new costume for the work—a tight-fitting bodice with bare shoulders, a thin muslin skirt, pink tights, and satin slippers. He eliminated almost all ornament; a little necklace, a bracelet, and a garland in the hair were enough for him. After the première, a "La Sylphide" hairdo was launched in one of the well-known hairdressing establishments of

* Théophile Gautier adds the comment: "Poor James. But why should we feel sorry for him? Because we can be sorry for all poets, dreamers, and young people with ideals."

the time, and ladies suddenly took to wearing clothing of thin muslin.

It is said that Véron could not sleep the night before the first performance because he was so concerned about the safety and smooth functioning of the technical apparatus that was to be used to enable the sylphs to "fly." But everything went off without a mishap; the ballet was a resounding success; and Marie Taglioni as the sylphid made her name one never to be forgotten.

The ballet was given in London on July 26, 1832, featuring Marie Taglioni as La Sylphide, Paul Taglioni as James, and Amalia Galster-Taglioni as Effie. In Denmark, the ballet was first presented on November 28, 1836, with Lucile Grahn in the title role and choreography by Auguste Bournonville; the ballet has been in the repertory of the Royal Danish Ballet ever since. *La Sylphide* was first presented in St. Petersburg on September 18, 1837, and in Milan on May 29, 1841. In December, 1945, it was presented by the Ballets des Champs-Elysées (staged by Victor Gsovsky), with Nina Vyroubova and Irène Skorik alternating in the title role, and with Roland Petit as James. On December 9, 1953, Harald Lander mounted the ballet for the Marquis de Cuevas Ballet première at the Empire Theater in Paris, with Rosella Hightower and Serge Golovine dancing the principal roles.

Giselle

Ballet in two acts. Book: Vernoy de Saint-Georges at the suggestion of Théophile Gautier, after a Central European folk fable recorded by Heinrich Heine. Choreography: Jules Perrot and Jean Coralli. Music: Adolphe Adam. Scenery: Ciceri. Première: June 28, 1841, at the Opéra, Paris.

CHARACTERS: Giselle; Count Albrecht, known to Giselle as Loys; Berthe, Giselle's mother; the Prince of Courlane; Wilfrid, Albrecht's squire; Hilarion, a gamekeeper; Bathilde, fiancée of Albrecht and daughter of the prince; Myrtha, the Queen of the Wilis; the prince's retinue; friends; hunters; Wilis.

❧

ACT I. As the curtain rises we see a landscape along the Rhine at vintage time. In the background are the outlines of a white-towered castle. In the left foreground is the cabin where Giselle lives with her mother. To the right is Albrecht's hut, where he lives disguised as a peasant. Albrecht has fallen in love with Giselle, but, since he is well aware that Giselle will not believe fine stories about shepherdesses who marry princes, he has changed his noble garb for that of a vintager and has given himself up to the greatest pleasure a young man can enjoy—being in love.

As the ballet begins, day is breaking. Hilarion appears and looks tenderly at Giselle's cottage. Before he can knock on the door, however, Albrecht (wearing a sword and cape over his peasant garb) and Wilfrid appear. Hilarion hides and watches the pair suspiciously. Wilfrid attempts to dissuade Albrecht from an un-disclosed project, but Albrecht does not listen. He gives his sword and cape to the squire and summarily dismisses him. Then he knocks on Giselle's door and playfully runs to hide. Giselle appears, radiantly happy, and does a little dance, for dancing is her passion; she dreams of partners who will not be easily tired out by a waltz. Annoyed at not finding Albrecht, Giselle proudly pretends not to care and dances again. Finally, Albrecht appears. At first Giselle feigns indifference to his presence, but later she tells him of her dream wherein she has seen him marrying a princess. Albrecht declares his undying devotion, but Giselle remains disturbed and to test his love plays "He loves me, he loves me not" with a daisy. When the game ends with "He loves me not," Giselle is distraught. Albrecht tells her fervently that every petal says, "He loves me." Giselle is reassured, and the two dance happily. Hilarion, who has secretly been observing this little rendezvous, emerges, pulls the two apart, and tells Albrecht to leave Giselle alone. Giselle angrily dismisses Hilarion, who shakes his fist at Albrecht as he leaves.

Village girls and boys now arrive with baskets of grapes and choose Giselle Queen of the Vintage. Giselle dances nimbly. But her mother warns: "Accursed child, you will become a Wili. You will die. You will appear in the nightly dance, with clothes the color of the moonlight, with bracelets of dewy pearls on your cold white arms. You will drag travelers into the deadly dance circle; you will throw them, panting and sweating, into the icy sea. You will become a vampire of the dance." Giselle answers these warnings as most girls would: "I'm not tired. One more dance, one more." She is too young, really, to believe in death, and the idea of dancing after death does not seem to terrify her; indeed, she thinks it would be more pleasant than to lie stiff and motionless within four wooden planks.

The sound of horns and barking dogs is heard in the valley, and a hunting party, consisting of the Prince of Courlane, his daughter, and a large retinue, enters. Albrecht, fearing an encounter with them, hastily leaves with the villagers. Giselle and her mother retire to their cottage. Hilarion, left alone, seizes the opportunity to search Albrecht's hut.

The princess is tired and thirsty and wants to rest in front of Giselle's cottage. She will drink some milk and eat the bread of the peasants—for such are the caprices of princesses!

Mother Berthe comes out of the cabin, leading Giselle. They bow low before the distinguished visitors. In the presence of such a noble lady, Giselle is a little shy. The princess is pretty and seems pleasant, and after Giselle has given Bathilde food and drink, she feels reassured. She comes close and, like an inquisitive kitten, timidly stretches out her hand to touch the richly ornamented clothing of the princess. Bathilde finds her charming and, with the gesture of a great lady, places a heavy gold chain around Giselle's neck. Flushed with pleasure, Giselle allows Bathilde to embrace her, not suspecting that this proud woman, smothered in the rustle of velvet and jewels, is her rival. The princess and her father then retire to the cottage to rest, and Albrecht returns with the villagers. He and Giselle are joyfully reunited in dance.

Hilarion chooses this moment to unmask his rival; he appears with Albrecht's cloak, sword, and spurs and shows them to Giselle, to the prince, to Bathilde, and to the retainers whom he has summoned from their rest; they immediately recognize the property of Count Albrecht, Bathilde's fiancé. As Giselle watches in horror, Bathilde walks over to Albrecht, who kneels at her feet.

Alas, poor Giselle, the man you loved was not what he seemed. A fatal chill envelops the girl for she has recognized Bathilde as the princess in her dream; she also realizes that great lords do not marry simple girls.

There is a maxim about women: *Coeur blessé, tête malade* ("Heart wounded, head sick"). Giselle loses her mind. She does not tear her hair like the heroines in melodramas; hers is a gentle madness, for she is a tender girl. She remembers her dance with Albrecht before she knew his true identity; she relives this dance, her feet going faster and faster. Then, as though she were again coming to her senses, she seizes the sword from Hilarion's hand and throws herself on its point. Albrecht snatches the sword away—too late. Giselle falls dead, her hand on her heart. Albrecht forces the remorseful Hilarion to look upon the dead girl, then falls weeping at her side.

ACT II. As the curtain rises we see a mysterious forest. Great trees with gnarled roots stand at the edge of a lake rimmed with reeds in which large water lilies are growing. A night breeze moves through the forest. The trees are bathed in a blue mist, and the light of the moon streams through the leaves. Sighs are heard. This is a spot no one ever visits. In a corner, some flowers and a stone cross mark a new grave. A beam of light reveals the name "Giselle" on the cross. Hunters seek temporary refuge here but are frightened away by Hilarion's tale of Wilis who dance here and who show no mercy to men.

A pale beautiful girl—Myrtha, the Queen of the Wilis—appears. With a scepter she points in the four directions of the compass. After all the Wilis have assembled, she summons Giselle, who rises stiffly from her grave. Released from the weight of the stone, she breathes deep. A star is fastened on her head, and two small transparent wings unfold on her shoulders. Giselle feels happy and free, like a butterfly, and she dances rapturously. After she finishes the dance, Myrtha, who hears someone approaching, bids the Wilis hide.

The leaves tremble as a hand parts them; Albrecht enters, sorrowfully. He has come to weep at Giselle's grave. He loved her truly, and it was only about his birth that he had deceived her. Giselle is deeply moved. She sighs, and Albrecht turns around and sees her gleaming blue eyes. He stretches out his arms to her, but he can only clasp the bulrushes and vines. Giselle appears again, and the two dance together once more. The Wilis return, and Giselle, knowing what will happen to her beloved should they find him, tries to conceal him. The Wilis are temporarily distracted by the return of Hilarion who, troubled by remorse, has lost his way and has come back to Giselle's grave. The Wilis surround him. His legs give way, and he breathes with great difficulty. He begs for mercy, but none is granted. Weary and at the end of his strength, he is turned round and round, thrust down the line of Wilis, and thrown into the lake. The water froths and boils; two or three rings are seen. Justice has been done.

The Wilis now discover Albrecht. "Leave me my Loys," Giselle cries. "Do not let him die, but let him see the light so that he may remember me and weep on my grave." "No, no, he must dance and die!" say the Wilis. "Don't listen to them, Loys! Hold fast to the cross on my grave; don't let it go. Myrtha's magic wand will break upon touching it." "That is so," Myrtha replies, "but you, Giselle, are subject to my will. I order you to do the fastest and the most voluptuous of dances and to display your loveliest smiles. Then Albrecht will leave the cross of his own free will!" Giselle begins her dance. The night will soon be over, and the cock will crow; time is of the essence. Albrecht remains at the grave, and Myrtha forces Giselle to put more force and energy into her dance. As she does so, Albrecht, unable to resist her any longer, joins her in a *pas de deux* and seems surely doomed. The Wilis force him to dance faster; Albrecht turns pale and is about to fall into the water. A clock in the distance strikes four. It is getting light, and the Wilis run off among the water lilies and into the hollows of trees. Albrecht is saved. As Giselle falls on the grass, the flowers bend over her. Her hand waves farewell, and then it disappears; the earth takes its prey. Albrecht searches frantically for her, in vain. All that he has left is a rose plucked from the grave. He falls exhausted into the arms of Bathilde and Wilfrid, who have been searching for him.*

* According to an old legend, still current in many parts of Europe, Wilis are said to be young girls who die before they can marry, and who rise up at night to continue the dance and pursue the pleasures they were deprived of so early. Woe to the young man who meets them! He is made to dance until he dies from exhaustion.

There is something peculiar about the Wilis. They are not at all the

☙

Whereas programs and reference works formerly cited Coralli as the choreographer for *Giselle,* it is now generally believed that Jules Perrot prepared the choreography for Giselle herself, a role danced at the première by Perrot's wife, Carlotta Grisi. Perrot's name, however, was neither on the poster nor in the program for the first performance. It had been forgotten or left out—an omission that can be attributed perhaps to the fact that Théophile Gautier was in love with Perrot's wife.

Giselle, along with *Swan Lake* and *Les Sylphides,* belongs to the group of ballets which a ballet company generally must produce to gain international recognition, and the success with which a company presents these works forms one of the standards which ballet critics use in order to measure excellence. This ballet has remained of great importance down to the present day.

Of the many revivals of *Giselle,* none has followed precisely the choreography and stage directions of the first performance. The steps have been altered and adapted to the individual techniques of the soloist. At the première the Prince of Courlane and Bathilde appeared on stage on horseback, and Myrtha was drawn across the stage on a plank with wheels so that she might keep a prettier balance. In the first act, the scene of the Bacchus-like figure on a wine vat has long since disappeared. The problem of reconstructing old ballets immediately raises the question of "authenticity." Restoring a scene known to have been per-

charming creatures in the airy tutus that one might imagine. Serge Lifar, the Russian expatriate who has had a long and successful career in France as dancer, choreographer, and author, reports that the Wilis are characters out of an old Serbian legend, in which, however, they are not girls who die before marriage, but wives who take revenge—sort of goddesses of vengeance. From a psychological point of view, this makes sense; it is hard to imagine that a girl who dies young would really revenge herself on young men. It is easy to think that she would like to keep dancing after death because it was such a joy while she was alive. Apparently the Wilis originally belonged to the legendary seductive women from the Germanic-Slavic world of the imagination who, under the influence of Christianity, were turned into dangerous beings who lead men to ruin.

formed in the nineteenth century but obviously theatrically inef-fective in the twentieth century may be "authentic," but it is not "good theater."

The Bolshoi Ballet performance of *Giselle* is probably one of the best. Leonid Lavrovsky, the choreographer responsible for this setting, worked from data derived from Petipa, Perrot, and Coralli. In the Bolshoi production Giselle is a simple country girl in love with Albrecht (Loys), whom she believes to be a peasant like herself. She is greatly disappointed when he is un-masked, and she, too, goes through the so-called mad scene, al-though without melodrama. The great difference in conception between the Russian version and others is in the characters of Hilarion and Albrecht. In the Bolshoi Ballet, Hilarion is a young farmer whose main role is to act indignant over Albrecht's deceit. To be sure, he is in love with Giselle, but most of all he wants to open her eyes to the sorrows that await her if she falls in love with Albrecht, the weakling who dares not reveal his real situa-tion. In the Bolshoi Ballet version, Albrecht is permitted to love the simple country girl, but he is not allowed to seduce her. In the usual productions in Western Europe and America, Albrecht is not so weak a figure, and Hilarion is depicted as a jealous youth who acts as an informer.

From its inception the role of Giselle has been a test of the ballerina's technical ability and her talent in pantomime. The role was danced in London in 1842 by Carlotta Grisi, in St. Petersburg in 1842 by Elena Andreyanova, and in Boston in 1846 by Mary Ann Lee. There have been many memorable interpreters of Giselle, among them Fanny Cerito (1843), Fanny Elssler (1843), Nadezhda Bogdanova (1856), Zina Mérante (1863), Anna Pavlova (1903), Thamar Karsavina (1910), Galina Ulanova (1932), Alicia Markova (1934), Margot Fonteyn (1937), Yvette Chauviré (1944), and Svetlana Beriosova (1956).

Giselle was the first ballet that truly made both lyric and dramatic demands on the ballerina, and the role has been coveted by every ballerina since, just as every *premier danseur* has wanted to dance Albrecht. Although the content of the ballet stamps it as something melodramatic, illogical, and internally and externally improbable, it still ranks as a touchstone for the ability of a ballerina, for in few other ballets can an individual dancer attain an equally admirable role both in the dramatic pantomime of the first act and in the romantic dance poetry of the second. For this reason *Giselle* has remained what it always was: a ballet which we admire not so much for itself as for the ballerina!

Napoli

Ballet in three acts. Book and choreography: Auguste Bournonville. Music: Paulli, E. Helsted, and N. W. Gade. Scenery: Christensen. Première: March 29, 1842, at the Royal Theater, Copenhagen.

CHARACTERS: Gennaro, a young fisherman; Veronica, a widow; Teresina, her daughter; Ambrosio, a monk; Giacomo, a macaroni vendor; Peppo, a lemonade vendor; Giovanina Pascarillo, a street singer; Carlina, a puppeteer; Golfo, a spirit of the sea; Coralla and Argentina, naiads; tritons; fishermen; country women; girls; children; naiads.

❧

ACT I. The Bay of Naples. Evening. Lamps shine along the quays and kitchen fires glow. A staircase, left, leads to Veronica's house.

A beggar is asleep in the foreground; men are playing a game; children are roasting chestnuts; and others are peeling oranges. Mothers are playing games with their children, and young girls are spinning. Giacomo's macaroni shop and Peppo's lemonade stand are heavily patronized. A tarantella is danced to a tambourine.

Teresina and her mother come on the stage. Giacomo and Peppo clearly show their love for the young girl, but Teresina's heart is out at sea, where her lover Gennaro is fishing. Each suitor courts the mother and tries to convince her that he is the right choice for Teresina. But the mother indicates that they have to settle the matter among themselves.

A barcarolle announces the return of the fishermen. The nets are hauled in by torchlight. There is great interest in the catch.

Gennaro embraces Teresina. The mother's conduct clearly shows that she prefers the wealthier suitors. The fishermen quarrel over the distribution of the catch, for Gennaro has placed the greatest share in front of the Madonna.

Brother Ambrosio appears and asks for alms. Some give him trifles; others turn their backs. Gennaro, however, does not forget the monk, and Teresina gives him a silver heart for his altar. Ambrosio blesses the young couple.

While Gennaro takes care of his fish, the two rivals try to make Teresina jealous and tell her that her marriage to Gennaro will be unlucky. Gennaro presents Teresina with a gold ring, and their betrothal is confirmed. Peppo and Giacomo continue their efforts to part the lovers, but Veronica finally gives her consent to their marriage and goes inside. The young lovers plan to talk over the future out on the bay; Teresina takes her guitar along and they row away.

Pascarillo sings some songs for the crowd, and Carlino shows off his puppets. Suddenly a storm comes up. Everyone looks for refuge. The fishermen draw their boats up on the bank, and in the distance Gennaro desperately tries to reach shore. The other fishermen rush to help. Gennaro returns unconscious; Teresina is not with him. When Gennaro revives, he asks at once for Teresina. Thereupon Veronica makes him feel that he alone is responsible for Teresina's death. Cursed by everyone and left alone, he throws himself before the image of the Madonna and implores her help. Brother Ambrosio joins him. The monk tells him to search in the sea and gives him a medallion which bears a miniature of the Madonna. Gennaro rows out to sea. The monk kneels in prayer.

Act II. A blue grotto.

Golfo, a spirit of the sea, comes out of the grotto. Tritons attend him. They hand him the treasures they have gathered, but Golfo shows little interest. An exotic melody is heard, and the naiads Argentina and Corallo sail in on a huge shell bearing Teresina and her guitar. Other naiads come close. They bring Teresina to the shore and lay her down on a bed of seaweed. Golfo is enchanted by her beauty. With the power of certain sea winds, Coralla brings Teresina back to life. Teresina is frightened at the sight of all the strange faces; she is sad and begs Golfo to let her return to Naples. Golfo, however, changes her into a naiad by pouring some water from the grotto over her, whereupon she loses all memory of the past. Coralla and Argentina adorn her with lovely jewels. Teresina throws her guitar away and picks up a shell and blows into it. At the sound, the naiads and tritons begin to dance. Golfo offers to share his kingdom and wealth with her but Teresina is unable to give him her love.

A boat approaches the grotto. Gennaro is looking for his beloved. When he discovers Teresina's guitar he knows she must be here. Golfo roars loudly, whereupon flames shoot from the fissures in the rocks. Gennaro is unafraid. He calls out to Teresina and speaks to her of his love, but she does not seem to recognize him. In desperation he takes up the guitar and shows her the medallion which he hangs around her neck. Teresina's memory returns slowly. Finally, she recognizes her lover and falls into his arms. As they are about to leave the grotto, Golfo stands in a towering rage in their way. He orders the naiads to seize Teresina and the tritons to lock up Gennaro in the grotto. Teresina succeeds in breaking away and clings to Gennaro. She raises the medallion and begs the spirits of the sea to submit to divine power. Golfo obeys and allows the pair to leave. The naiads place the jewels in the boat with them, and the reunited couple heads homeward.

ACT III. Monte Virginia, outside Naples. Noon. A picture of the Madonna hangs on the center pier of a bridge connecting two hills. The Bay of Naples and the volcano Vesuvius are visible through the arches of the bridge.

Pilgrims and children carrying banners cross the bridge. When they reach level ground, they kneel before the picture of the Madonna. The women rise and decorate the Madonna with flowers. A conversation concerning Teresina's absence ensues. Peppo repeats his prophecy, and Giacomo tells tales about young girls carried away by dark powers.

Then Teresina, Veronica, and Gennaro arrive. Teresina, overwhelmed with questions, tells how Gennaro saved her. Veronica is afraid that Gennaro has the power of witchcraft and feels that it is her duty to part the happy couple. Gennaro becomes furious over this sudden turn of events. The spectators are frightened by his outburst, and soldiers are called to calm him. But they, too, are afraid of sorcery and drop their weapons. Finally, a monk is summoned to combat the evil spirits. The crowd follows him with curiosity, but at a safe distance. Suddenly the monk stops and stretches out his arms; everyone sees that he is Ambrosio. He explains that Teresina was saved by the medallion of the Madonna dell'Arco. The tension subsides, and gaiety takes its place. Even Peppo and Giacomo wish the young couple good fortune. All dance with joy.

Young men unhitch the horses of a wagon, which they bedeck with flowers as a triumphal chariot for Gennaro and his bride, and pull the couple home, in a joyous bacchanal.

Auguste Bournonville the choreographer of *Napoli* preferred the true dance, and so most of his ballets are characterized by a large number of dances. For *Napoli* he made a long visit to Italy to record customs and dances. At the première he danced the part of Gennaro himself. The ballet is still popular in Denmark. Harald Lander mounted a shortened version of *Napoli*, combining dances from the various acts, for the London Festival Ballet in 1954. Scenery and costumes were by Osbert Lancaster; Toni Lander and Oleg Briansky danced the principal roles.

La Esmeralda

Ballet in three acts, five scenes. Book (from Victor Hugo's Notre Dame de Paris) *and choreography: Jules Perrot. Music: Cesare Pugni. Scenery: W. Grieve. Costumes: Copère; Stage machinery: D. Sloman. Première: March 9, 1844, at Her Majesty's Theatre, London.*

CHARACTERS: La Esmeralda, a street dancer; Phoebus de Chateaupers, the fiancé of Fleur de Lys; Fleur de Lys; Madame Aloise de Gondelaurier, mother of Fleur de Lys; Diane and Beranger, friends of Fleur de Lys; Claude Frollo; Pierre Gringoire, a poet; Quasimodo, the bell ringer of Notre Dame; Clopin Trouillefou; rogues.

ACT I. The rendezvous of the underworld in fifteenth-century Paris. Sunset.

A number of shady characters, directed by Clopin, are assembled on a hill. While merriment is at its height, Gringoire runs in and falls at Clopin's feet; a band of thieves are about to rob him. Clopin makes Gringoire stand up, and when the poet realizes where he is, he shudders with fear. Several pickpockets search him but their only loot is a poem. Clopin, angered by so slight a "haul," orders the poet hanged. Gringoire begs for mercy while the vagabonds ridicule him. Clopin makes a jest of the matter and tells Gringoire he will spare his life if he can find a woman who will marry him; thereupon he orders the women who are present to come closer. They look Gringoire over, but all refuse to have him as a husband. Gringoire, blinded with fear, throws himself at their feet. Then La Esmeralda appears and, with feminine intuition, immediately comprehends the situation. She will marry Gringoire, she tells Clopin. An earthenware pot is brought in and set down in front of Gringoire, and La Esmeralda tells him to break it. The shards fly in all directions. Clopin unites the couple in wedlock, and the marriage is celebrated by a dance.

The gathering breaks up at the sound of vesper bells. Claude Frollo, who has been standing among the crowd watching La Esmeralda dance, is madly in love with her and tells Clopin that he wants to make her his that night. Clopin tells him where he can find her. Frollo takes Quasimodo with him and the two wait for La Esmeralda. They hear her light step. Frollo springs at her, and she struggles to get free. March music is heard; Phoebus and his police archers come on the scene just in time. La Esmeralda wrenches free; Frollo flees; and Quasimodo falls into the hands of Phoebus and the archers.

La Esmeralda looks at her handsome rescuer with growing interest. Phoebus in turn is struck by her beauty. In order to enjoy her company a little longer, he starts questioning her and finds out that she is an orphan. During the conversation La Esmeralda toys with the corner of the richly embroidered shawl Phoebus is wearing, and he presents it to her. At this moment La Esmeralda discovers that Quasimodo is about to faint and gives him some water from the jug she carries with her. At her request Phoebus orders the archers to set Quasimodo free. The hunchback leaves, thanking his benefactor. Phoebus thinks that La Esmeralda might well give him a kiss in exchange for her rescue. The gypsy girl refuses and tries to return his shawl. Phoebus seizes her, but she slips out of his arms and escapes. The frustrated warrior goes off at the head of his archers.

Act II, Scene 1. A small vaulted chamber with a chair, table, and bed.

La Esmeralda comes in. In her hand is Phoebus' shawl which she regards thoughtfully. She sits at the table and spells out the name of her beloved Phoebus in ivory letters. She is so absorbed in her act of love that she does not notice Gringoire enter the room. The poet looks at his wife in admiration. She is absent-minded, he thinks, because she is lost in tender thoughts about their marriage. He comes up to her stealthily and puts his arm around her waist. La Esmeralda is frightened and breaks away. Gringoire tries to catch her. Just as he is about to seize her, she takes a dagger from her belt and brandishes it before him. It is his turn to be afraid. La Esmeralda reveals that it was only out of pity that she married him, but if he wants to, he may accompany her in her street dancing—nothing more. He decides to be content with that. La Esmeralda begins to dance, but Gringoire finds it impossible to keep his promise. La Esmeralda is displeased and pushes him into an adjoining room, where Gringoire must reconcile himself to his lot.

La Esmeralda, alone, lies down to sleep. At this moment Frollo enters and, in a torrent of words, tells her how much he loves her. La Esmeralda tries to get him to leave her in peace and points to the name that she has spelled out on the table. Frollo becomes angry and attacks her. La Esmeralda calls Gringoire to help her. Frollo hears a sound and looks around. At this moment La Esmeralda escapes through a secret door. Frollo wants to follow her, but the door of Gringoire's room swings open, and the poet appears, pale, on the threshold. Frollo seizes his dagger and threatens to stab Gringoire if he comes a step closer. Quasimodo, who has observed the entire scene without any show of emotion, swears vengeance against Frollo.

Act II, Scene 2. The garden of the Gondelaurier family.

Preparations for the marriage between Fleur de Lys and Phoebus de Chateaupers are in progress. Fleur de Lys enters the garden with a group of girl friends who carry baskets with flowers to make garlands for the celebration. When Madame de Gondelaurier comes in, she is greeted respectfully. Fleur de Lys shows her what they are doing. Phoebus enters and gives his betrothed a hasty kiss. She notices that he is not wearing the shawl she had embroidered for him. The guests arrive and the festivities begin.

La Esmeralda appears with Gringoire. He accompanies her dance with tambourine and guitar. Fleur de Lys is astonished by La Esmeralda's beauty. The dancer says that she can read hands and foretell the future. Fleur de Lys gives her a ring and asks her to finish her dancing. Then La Esmeralda sees her beloved Phoebus, who seems to have forgotten his bride entirely. He invites La Esmeralda to dance with him, and she accepts his invitation. Fleur de Lys reproaches Phoebus for his unseemly conduct, to which he makes some cold excuses. La Esmeralda dances with Gringoire but allows Phoebus to see the shawl he had given her and which she is wearing to show her faithfulness. Fleur de Lys recognizes the shawl she had embroidered and takes it away from the dancer. She becomes so angry that she falls to the ground unconscious and is carried out. Gringoire has his hands full protecting La Esmeralda from the enraged guests, but he finally succeeds in taking her away. Phoebus hesitates an instant and then follows the pair.

ACT III, SCENE 1. A tavern with a window overlooking the Seine. Nighttime.

Clopin comes in with a torch in his hand; Frollo follows. Clopin shows him a hiding place and then leaves. Frollo, who has La Esmeralda's dagger; hides in wait. Phoebus and La Esmeralda enter, conversing tenderly. Phoebus declares his love for her. How is it possible, La Esmeralda asks, to love two people at once? She takes a feather from her plume and blows it into the air, to show what she thinks of his love. Then she kneels at his feet and looks adoringly up at him. Frollo, who has seen all this from his hiding place, can control his jealousy no longer; he rushes at the lovers with his dagger. Phoebus and La Esmeralda run into the back room. Frollo follows. A cry of pain is heard, and a body falls. Frollo walks out and disappears through the open window. La Esmeralda also comes out and faints. Passers-by enter the tavern. Clopin, who is among them, goes into the back room, discovers the body of Phoebus, and denounces La Esmeralda as the murderess. She protests her innocence, but no one believes her, and she is taken away.

ACT III, SCENE 2. The banks of the Seine. To the right, a prison; in the background, the towers of Notre Dame.

La Esmeralda is brought to prison by archers. A crowd follows. Soon Gringoire appears. He is appalled to hear that his wife has been condemned to the stake. He urges the crowd to try to prevent the execution, but the procession of the King of Fools comes along and he is swept away by the merrymakers. As La Esmeralda passes through the prison gate, the procession stops for a moment. Gringoire can see his wife clearly. La Esmeralda requests that Phoebus' shawl be burned with her. Frollo emerges from the mob and once more tries to seduce her by promising to save her life if she will marry him. La Esmeralda refuses, and Frollo gives the archers the order to go ahead. Suddenly Phoebus, who had been thought dead, appears; the blow had not been fatal. La Esmeralda faints at the sight of her lover. Phoebus kneels and swears that she is innocent, that it was Frollo who attempted to kill him. Now the archers take Frollo into custody. When the street dancer regains consciousness, she discovers Phoebus at her feet. Frollo can not endure the good fortune of the two lovers. He attacks La Esmeralda with a knife, but Quasimodo leaps to her defense, snatches the weapon, and plunges it into Frollo's breast.

The crowd rejoices because the street dancer has been proved to be innocent and will remain among them.

❧

At the première the roles of La Esmeralda, Phoebus, and Gringoire were danced by Carlotta Grisi, Arthur Saint-Léon, and Jules Perrot, respectively. In 1851 in Moscow Fanny Elssler chose this ballet for her farewell performance. During the first act she received more than 300 bouquets of flowers, which were arranged to form her bed and pillow in Act II. (Elssler, who was supposed to write out the name *Phoebus* in this act, changed it to *Moscow* for the occasion.) Since the role of La Esmeralda calls for perfect technique and great ability in pantomime, it is easy to understand why a ballerina such as Fanny Elssler would love to appear in it.

The Russian première took place in St. Petersburg on January 2, 1849, and the ballet is still in repertory.

Nicholas Beriosov mounted a version for the London Festival Ballet which was first performed at the Festival Hall, London, on July 15, 1954, with scenery and costumes by Nicola Benois. The principal dancers were Nathalie Krassovska, John Gilpin, Oleg Briansky, Belina Wright, Anton Dolin, and Keith Beckett.

Pas de Quatre

Divertissement. Choreography: Jules Perrot. Music: Cesare Pugni. Première: July 12, 1845, at Her Majesty's Theatre, London.

BALLERINAS: Marie Taglioni, Fanny Cerito, Lucile Grahn, and Carlotta Grisi. (Order is the same as on the original poster.)

As the curtain goes up, the four dancers enter and form a group centering around Marie Taglioni, whose arms are stretched up high. To the left Carlotta Grisi kneels; to the right is Lucile Grahn, with her arm on Taglioni's hip. Fanny Cerito is seated in the foreground. After the audience has had a chance to admire this grouping, it breaks up. The ballerinas greet each other with bows. Taglioni leads Cerito and Grisi from the stage. The first variation now begins: a *pas seul* by Grahn. Next comes a *pas seul* by Carlotta Grisi. Then, Cerito, who has been brought in by Taglioni and Grahn, executes a waltz. At the end of her dance she bows to Taglioni who dances her solo last. Finally the four renowned ballerinas dance a *pas de quatre* and finish with the famous finale position that Alfred Chalon recorded in a lithograph.

During the curtain call, to deafening applause, Cerito placed a crown of white roses on Taglioni's hair. The fan that she also presented to her colleague is still in perfect condition and is in the possession of Cyril Beaumont, British writer and dance critic.

This *divertissement*, which stirred all London and was a boon to the florists, was the idea of Benjamin Lumley, the director of Her Majesty's Theatre, who thought it would be an exciting experience to present the four great ballerinas of his time on stage together. (The fifth great ballerina of the day, Fanny Elssler, was too bitter a rival of Taglioni to be considered for such an occasion; in any event, she had previously appeared at Her Majesty's Theatre in a very successful *pas de deux* with Cerito.) Jules Perrot was chosen to arrange the dances, and this capable ballet master and choreographer excelled himself. Everything was organized magnificently, and each ballerina seemed satisfied with the dances given her. But, during the final rehearsal a quarrel broke out between two of the ballerinas. According to Taglioni, who was assigned without dispute to the number one position (i.e., the last variation), Cerito began the quarrel by arguing with Grisi about whose variation would precede Taglioni's. Each dancer stood firm, appealing to her own technical ability and popularity with the public. Perrot lacked the tact required to solve the dispute. Lumley, however, did not allow himself to be disconcerted. "In this dilemma there is one point on which the ladies must not be insincere," he said. "Let the oldest take her unquestionable right to the envied position." Perrot went back and made the proposal. The trick worked; the dancers laughed; and everything was in order. In 1847 Lucile Grahn was replaced by Carolina Rosati; but the *divertissement* remained just as successful.

The English choreographer Keith Lester devised a version of *Pas de Quatre* that has been in the repertory of many companies since 1936. Anton Dolin fashioned another version which was first presented by the Ballet Theatre in New York on February 16, 1941, by the Festival Ballet in Monte Carlo on May 21, 1951, and by the Royal Danish Ballet in Copenhagen in 1955. In a performance staged by the Ballet Russe de Monte Carlo in New York in 1948, the interpreters were Alicia Markova (Taglioni), Nathalie Krassovska (Grahn), Mia Slavenska (Grisi), and Alexandra Danilova (Cerito).

In recent years, this famous work by Perrot has been used as a showcase for promising young dancers. Although we can not fully envisage the dexterity and charms of the ballerinas of 1845, we may assume that the young aspirants will have their work cut out for them in trying to reach the level of Taglioni, Cerito, Grahn, and Grisi.

Coppélia

Ballet in two acts, three scenes. Book: Charles Nuitter and Arthur Saint-Léon. Choreography: Arthur Saint-Léon. Music: Léo Delibes. Scenery: Cambon, Despléchin, and Lavaster. Costumes: Paul Lormier. Première: May 25, 1870, at the Opéra, Paris.

CHARACTERS: Swanilda; Coppélia, a doll; Franz, Swanilda's beloved; Dr. Coppélius, the dollmaker; the mayor; the lord of the castle; mechanical dolls; allegorical figures connected with the dedication of the bells; nobles; pages; countryfolk.

ACT I. Market place of a frontier town in Galicia. To the left, the house of Swanilda; to the right, the house of Dr. Coppélius.

After a brief overture, the curtain rises. Swanilda comes out of her house and steals over to the house of Dr. Coppélius. She looks up at the big balcony window, where a very beautiful girl, Coppélia, said to be Dr. Coppélius' daughter, is sitting motionless with a book. Swanilda is jealous of the girl because she thinks that Franz, her lover, is paying her too much attention. She tries to get the girl's attention but does not succeed. Hearing footsteps, Swanilda quickly hides. Franz arrives and goes to Swanilda's house —reluctantly. His glance travels to the beautiful Coppélia to whom he blows a kiss. Coppélia turns her head toward him. She stands up, seems to blow his kiss back, and suddenly sits down. Swanilda, who has been watching all the time, comes out, pretending to chase a butterfly. Franz joins her in the chase, catches a butterfly, and pins it to his lapel. Swanilda begins to scold him for his conduct, asking him whether he cares for Coppélia or for her. Franz protests that he is innocent, but Swanilda declares she will have nothing more to do with him.

A group of young people come in dancing, and Swanilda joins in a mazurka, even though she is still angry with Franz.

When the mayor enters, he reports that the lord of the castle has presented the town with a clock that will be dedicated the next day; couples married on the same day will receive a dowry from the lord. The mayor asks Swanilda in a whisper whether she will be one of them. "Not yet," Swanilda replies. She takes a stalk from a sheaf of corn, holds it to her ear, and listens. The stalk apparently tells her that Franz is not faithful, for she breaks it in two. Franz leaves in a bad mood. Swanilda then dances with the other girls to a Slavic folk melody. The girls dance a czardas with the young men. All leave by couples.

Dr. Coppélius comes out of his house, closing the door carefully behind him. As he tries to cross the square, he is detained by a group of youths who ridicule him. In the scuffle that ensues, Coppélius unwittingly drops his door key. He frees himself finally and leaves, denouncing the youths who have accosted him.

Swanilda, returning home, finds the door key and shows it to the other girls, who thereupon propose a visit to the mysterious house of Dr. Coppélius. They do not hesitate very long. Swanilda unlocks the door, and she and her friends enter.

Franz appears with a ladder, which he places against Coppélia's balcony. He wants to know Coppélia better. He starts up the ladder, then hesitates a moment to look toward Swanilda's house and to think how cruel she has been to him. At that moment Dr. Coppélius, having discovered that his key is lost, returns and finds Franz on the ladder. Franz manages to jump down and flee. Dr. Coppélius then notices that the door to his house is open; he hurries in.

ACT II, SCENE 1. The dollmaker's workshop. All kinds of tools and equipment for making mechanical dolls are lying around. Dolls are everywhere, either standing or sitting. The room is dimly lit by a lamp.

Swanilda and her friends enter the room fearfully and notice the various dolls. Swanilda goes to the curtain behind which she believes Coppélia must be sitting. She pulls the curtain back and Coppélia is revealed, still sitting there with the book in her hand. Swanilda begins to talk to her, but there is no answer. Timidly, she touches Coppélia's arm; it is cold. She puts her hand on Coppélia's heart; it is not beating. So, Coppélia is a doll! The girls are delighted by this revelation. No longer afraid, they begin to set all the dolls in motion. Just then, Dr. Coppélius comes storming in. He stops the dolls and drives the girls out. Swanilda hides behind the curtain. After the girls have disappeared, Coppélius inspects Coppélia, who is still sitting undisturbed on her chair behind the curtain. Coppélius hears a noise outside. He goes to the window and sees Franz coming up the ladder again. Coppélius hides in order to trap Franz. Franz enters, and when he is well inside, Coppélius bars the way. Franz declares that he is in love with the beauty, Coppélia. Coppélius says he can understand that and proposes that they drink a glass of wine together. Franz accepts. Coppélius mixes a soporific drug into the wine, but he himself does not drink. He watches the drink take effect. Franz tries once more to reach Coppélia, but his feet fail him. He totters and falls in a deep sleep upon a chair.

Coppélius then brings out his book of magic formulas, and after reading (in pantomime) a number of them, he opens the curtain and rolls out the chair with his doll. It appears that he wants to use his incantations to make himself master of Franz's soul in order to give it to his doll. Coppélia rises from her chair, drops the book, and takes one step, then another. Gradually she loses her rigidity and begins to laugh and dance. She sees the wine and wants to drink it, but Coppélius manages to snatch it from her. She sees the book of magic formulas and tries to open it with her toes. She finds a sword and runs it through one of the dolls, then threatens to do the same to Franz. The old man hurries after her, succeeds in regaining the sword, and tries to pacify her with pretty things. With a mantilla draped around her, she does a Spanish dance. Next she finds a Scottish shawl, wraps it around her, and does a Scottish dance. Meanwhile, Franz has begun to regain consciousness. Dr. Coppélius finally manages to get his "doll" (everyone now realizes that it is Swanilda, who is wearing Coppélia's clothing) in back of the curtain again and then ejects Franz through the window. He wants to stop Coppélia's mechanism and draws the curtain aside. Coppélia is sitting in her former position. Swanilda takes advantage of the situation to slip out of the room; on the way she sets two mechanical dolls in motion.

Through the window, Dr. Coppélius catches a glimpse of Swanilda escaping with Franz and realizes that a trick has been played on him. Exhausted and defeated, he falls down in the midst of his dolls, who remorselessly continue their mechanical movements.

Act II, Scene 2. A field outside the lord's castle. The clock to be dedicated is suspended from poles decorated with flags. In front of the clock is a wagon on which are allegorical figures. A platform is set up for the lord of the castle. Guards maintain order.

The priests dedicate the clock. Then they present to the lord those couples who will marry that day and who will thus receive a dowry. Franz and Swanilda decide at the last moment to marry. Dr. Coppélius rushes in to demand payment for the damage which Franz, Swanilda, and her friends have done in his house. Who is going to pay for the damage? Swanilda, who has already received her dowry from the lord, gives it to Coppélius, but the lord says that he will make good the loss and that she should keep her dowry. He pays Coppélius full damages and mounts the platform. Now, the festivities can begin.

The bell ringer steps down from the wagon and announces the morning hours. Twelve girls dance the waltz of the hours. Then Aurora, goddess of the morning, appears; she is surrounded by the field flowers. Hour of Prayer enters, blesses the day, and departs. Time passes, and Aurora and the Morning Hours leave the field. The day's work must begin: Spinners and harvesters begin their chores. A procession enters and Hymen, the god of marriage, appears, accompanied by Cupid. The marriage festivities, however, are disturbed by the alarm bell. Fire glows in the heavens; there is War and Discord. Fortunately Peace soon returns with an olive branch in her hand. Calm is restored as evening and night hours bring joy.

After this allegorical interlude on the function and significance of the clock, the moment has come for a great festival of joy. Following an adagio by Franz and Swanilda, all dance a galop as the finale.

❧

In 1866 Charles Nuitter, archivist of the Paris Opéra, took the subject for this ballet from E. T. A. Hoffmann's *Der Sandmann* in order to create a ballet for the dancer Léontine Beaugrand. Delibes composed the music, and rehearsals were begun. But Perrin, the director of the Opéra, was afraid that Beaugrand would not attract a sufficiently large audience and insisted on a Russian ballerina to take the title role. For this purpose Adele Grantsova came from Russia, but the rehearsals took so much time that her contract expired before the ballet was performed. Perrin looked for another dancer, and this time chose the sixteen-year-old Italian, Giuseppina Bozacchi. The première took place after three years of preparation and achieved an immediate success before an audience including the emperor and his retinue. Soon after the première the Franco-Prussian War broke out, and Bozacchi died during the siege of Paris. On October 16, 1871, Beaugrand finally stepped into the role conceived for her. Eugénie Fiocre, a ballerina, originally danced the role of Franz, and the role has been played by a woman in subsequent French revivals.

The ballet contains a great deal of pantomime and is given in various versions. Small ballet groups often give only the so-called Doll Act, where all that is needed is one good ballerina and some mimes. Often, the entire allegorical portion in the last scene is not performed. Also, the lord and his retinue are, usually without explanation, omitted. This does violence to the original libretto and makes the third scene incomprehensible, for it is precisely the dedication of the clock by the priests and the presentation of the marriage gifts to all the couples by the lord of the castle that comprises the framework of the story. The mayor is watchful of the interests of his fellow-citizens and therefore urges Swanilda to get married, too—as if to say one shouldn't let a dowry get away!

In Russia the première took place at St. Petersburg on November 25, 1884, with Varvara Nikitina in the title role.

In the English première on May 14, 1906, Adeline Genée danced the title role. Subsequently, *Coppélia* became one of the most popular ballets in England. The first performance of the Vic-Wells Ballet occurred on March 21, 1933, at the Sadler's Wells Theatre, London, with Lydia Lopokova as Coppélia. This version (Act I and Act II, Scene 1, as described in this book) was constructed by Nicholas Sergeyev, after Ivanov and Cecchetti. Act III (Act II, Scene 2) was restored in the performance on April 15, 1940.

The Ballet Russe de Monte Carlo presented a large-scale revival staged by Sergeyev (American première, October 17, 1938) with Alexandra Danilova as Coppélia. Many have considered Danilova the finest interpreter of the role, in which she had as partners, among others, Frederic Franklin and Igor Youskevitch.

The Sadler's Wells Theatre Ballet mounted a full-length version for the première on September 4, 1951, at the Sadler's Wells Theatre. On March 2, 1954, the Sadler's Wells staged a new production under the supervision of Ninette de Valois, with Nadia Nerina in the title role.

Sylvia*

Ballet in three acts, four scenes. Book: Jules Barbier and Baron de Reinach. Choreography: Louis Mérante. Music: Léo Delibes. Scenery: Chéret, Rubé, and Chaperon. Costumes: Eugène Lacoste. Première: June 14, 1876, at the Opéra, Paris.

CHARACTERS: Sylvia; Diana; Eros; Amyntas, a shepherd; Orion, a hunter; two slaves; nymphs; satyrs; naiads; dryads; shepherds and shepherdesses; country men and women; bacchants; pages of Bacchus; slaves.

⌘

ACT I. A clearing in a forest. Moonlight. To the left stands a statue of Eros, surrounded by a semicircle of columns. To the right of the statue a staircase leads into the forest; and further to the right branches overhang a brook.

The forest folk are having fun. Dryads emerge from the water. Fauns attempt to catch the dryads who, laughing, succeed in eluding them. The fauns try to hold the dryads with garlands of flowers. At the sound of approaching footsteps, all run off into hiding.

Amyntas, the shepherd, appears. He listens keenly but hears nothing. He puts down his shepherd's staff, takes off his cloak, and in a reverie sits down. Some time ago in this clearing he saw a beautiful girl. Her picture is still engraved on his heart, and he hopes against hope that he may see her again. Was she one of Diana's nymphs, whom he cannot love with an earthly love?

* See page 169 for a contemporary version.

The sound of horns is heard. Amyntas hides behind the statue of Eros. He waits anxiously. Sylvia enters with her nymphs, and they dance to honor the hunt. It seems that they are challenging Eros in the name of their chaste goddess Diana. Some of them are tired and lie down to rest, others play, and some bathe in the brook. Sylvia swings to and fro on a strong branch. Orion, the dark hunter, enters. When he sees the nymphs, he hides and secretly watches them.

Suddenly, one of the nymphs sees the staff and cloak of Amyntas Indignant at the thought that they are being spied on, the nymphs seek the owner, find Amyntas, and drag him to Sylvia. At the same time Orion comes forward threateningly; he will not tolerate any rival for Sylvia's affection.

When Amyntas sees his beloved Sylvia, he forgets the situation he is in. For a moment, Sylvia considers shooting him with an arrow, but relents. He is a mere mortal whose feelings are attributable to Eros. It is Eros whom she must strike. She lets loose the arrow. Amyntas springs between her and the statue to shelter the god of love, and Sylvia's arrow strikes Amyntas, who falls, smiling, at her feet. The nymph looks on unmoved. Now Eros comes to life and looses a golden arrow at Sylvia which strikes her in the heart. She stands trembling for an instant, her hand over her heart, while her friends hasten to see whether she is wounded. She shakes her head, pulls out the arrow, and places it into her quiver.

Day breaks. Sounds of bagpipes and a drum draw closer. Sylvia blows on her horn and disappears into the woods with her nymphs. The sun lights up the treetops. Young men and women, passing by on their way to the harvest, kneel for an instant before the statue of Eros. Shepherdesses with jugs and baskets follow. Orion enters, glad that Amyntas has fallen and is no longer a rival. He devises a plan to seize the nymph with a golden chain and quickly hides when he hears footsteps.

Sylvia returns, looking for Amyntas. She draws the golden arrow from her quiver and presses it on Amyntas' lips. Orion comes close and throws the chain, but the nymph escapes. After a short chase he catches her and carries her off.

A young shepherd, who has remained behind in hiding and has observed the abduction, now summons his friends. Together they try unsuccessfully to revive Amyntas. An old sorcerer appears and presses a rose to Amyntas' lips. The youth regains consciousness and becomes distraught over news of his vanished love. The sorcerer tries to comfort him, saying that Sylvia might have been wounded by one of Eros's arrows. Amyntas approaches Eros and observes that the god's bow is no longer bent. Amyntas then asks the sorcerer whether or not he knows where Sylvia is. The sorcerer answers that cries in the distance indicate she has been taken captive. At this instant the shepherds return with Sylvia's cloak, and Amyntas swears to liberate his love. Before leaving, however, he turns to the statue of Eros, which is suddenly transformed into the living god of love. The shepherds kneel before Eros as he stands in the blaze of the sun's rays. Eros points out the way, and Amyntas departs on his quest to free Sylvia.

Act II. A dark grotto with a narrow entrance. To the right, a passage leads to another part of the grotto. Blocks of stone serve as chairs and tables.

Sylvia is asleep on a bed of moss. Orion hangs her bow and quiver on the wall. As he stands looking at his captive, Sylvia slowly opens her eyes. Seeing Orion, she shrieks and tries to escape from the grotto. Orion quickly blocks her way. She threatens him with the vengeance of Diana and tries again to escape from the grotto. Orion takes a rock and closes the entrance. He declares his love for her, but she refuses him. Then he orders nourishment, and two slaves bring in fruit and some drink. Sylvia, however, asks the slaves to press the juice from the grapes. She pours the liquor for Orion and herself. To pass the time, she executes a bacchanalian dance and afterwards offers Orion some more of the liquor. Orion then tries to take Sylvia in his arms, but his senses are clouded. He falls asleep, and Sylvia once more seeks to escape from the grotto. She finds her bow and quiver and begs Eros for help. The god appears and leads her out of Orion's grotto. At a sign from Eros the entire grotto sinks into the earth; Sylvia expresses her gratitude to the god. The sound of a horn is heard in the distance; Sylvia is anxious to return to her friends. Eros tells her what has happened to Amyntas and how he now sadly waits for her.

Act III. A forest by the seaside. To the left, a temple of Diana. In the distance, mountains.

Countryfolk enter with pictures of Bacchus and Silenus. The

image of Bacchus is placed on an improvised altar (an oak stump),
that of Silenus, nearby. The girls make offerings of grapes and
dance a bacchanal.

Amyntas returns from his unsuccessful search for Sylvia, and the
girls try to console him. Then a ship is sighted, which slowly approaches the shore. Eros, disguised as a pirate, disembarks, followed by a number of slaves. Amyntas starts to leave but is held
by one of the slave girls. When she removes her veil, he recognizes
his beloved Sylvia, and, overcome with joy, falls at her feet. The
reunion is short-lived, however, for the wicked Orion appears,
bearing an ax, and attacks the couple. Amyntas throws his staff
at him, and Sylvia flees into the temple of Diana. Diana closes
the door of the temple, and Orion attacks the temple door with
his ax. The countryfolk draw back in terror. It grows darker
as threatening clouds gather; thunder can be heard. At the third
thunderclap the door of the temple opens. Diana stands on the
threshold with bent bow; Sylvia kneels next to her. The nymphs,
standing in groups around the temple, watch. Orion leaps at Sylvia,
but in the same instant Diana's arrow strikes the hunter, killing
him. Clouds hide the temple.

Diana now asks Sylvia how she happened to lose her friends.
Sylvia tells the goddess of her wanderings, of Eros, and of her
wound. She also discloses her love for Amyntas. The lovers beseech
forgiveness, but Diana refuses.

As a thunderclap reverberates, all bow their heads in fear. Eros,
still in the garb of a pirate, asks Diana why she is so inexorable.
He produces magically a vision of her visiting the sleeping En-
dymion, whereupon Diana is amazed that a mortal should know
the secrets of the gods. Eros thereupon shows his true form. Diana
forgives Sylvia and Amyntas.

Sunlight streams through a break in the clouds. The temple
of Diana appears once more. Diana withdraws into the background,
followed by her nymphs, and smiles on the pair who bow low in
her honor. The countryfolk look on in wonder.

Sylvia has everything in it: gods, shepherds, and countryfolk. In a way, the ballet came a hundred years too late, for we

know its ingredients from the time of the shepherdesses and the Rococo. In a sense it is more preromantic—or else a return to the preromantic because the romantic was dying.

At the première Mérante, the choreographer, himself danced the role of Amyntas, with Rita Sangalli as Sylvia. Orion was interpreted by the Italian M. Magri, and Marie Sanlaville must have been enchanting in her role of Eros. The costumes by Lacoste and the music of Delibes were greatly admired.

The ballet entered the repertory in St. Petersburg on December 15, 1901, with Olga Preobrajenska in the roll of Sylvia. A lavish production of *Sylvia,* choreographed by Frederick Ashton and designed by Robin and Christopher Ironside, was presented by Sadler's Wells Ballet in London on September 3, 1952, with Margot Fonteyn in the title role.

4

Glory in Russia, Decline in France

Russia, and especially St. Petersburg, was to develop the art of ballet further—with the help of Frenchmen and other foreigners. In France, the ballet declined, perhaps because public interest shifted to painting, which experienced a new flowering, and to the minor arts. But in Russia, the art of ballet reached new heights. Notable among those working in St. Petersburg during the last half of the nineteenth century were Jules Perrot (who arrived in 1848), Mazilier (the least successful of the "foreign invaders," who came there in 1851), Marius Petipa (the descendant of a clan of dancers, instructor at the Imperial School in 1854), Arthur Saint-Léon (who worked with the ballet more or less continuously from 1859 to 1869) and a native Russian, Lev Ivanov (who became second ballet master under Petipa in 1885). The leading personality in ballet at this time was Marius Petipa,* chief choreographer of the Imperial Ballet from 1862 to 1903. His work—about sixty ballets are credited to him—set the tone for this era.

* The name is a phonetically simplified form of petipas—small step.

Various theories have been propounded to explain the causes which led to the glory of the Russian ballet. Some critics point to the earnestness with which the Russians do everything, to their enormous dedication and perseverance—characteristics attributed today to the Bolshoi Ballet of Moscow, the Stanislavsky Ballet of Leningrad, and the Kirov Ballet of Leningrad (formerly the Maryinsky Ballet, St. Petersburg).

But the *real* explanation, it seems to me, for both the decline of the French and the rise of the Russian ballet, lies chiefly in social relationships. In France, industrialization and mechanization had made greater inroads on craftsmanship. In artistic circles it was not what man did with his hands, but what machines could do for man, that became significant. The Eiffel Tower is the symbol of the age. What man himself did and could do with machine-made products was "business," and "business" was what he did with everything and everyone, including himself. For many artists it was no longer technical skill that was important in ballet, and still less the expression of inner feelings (as in early Romanticism), but the exhibition and sale of female beauty and erotic charm. That meant the end of French ballet art, and, with the exception of isolated revivals, it has remained the end of it. In Russia, however, the people remained serious about creative work, and here, during the first half of the nineteenth century, the ballet could begin its great age as a craft.

What Petipa did was to introduce and extend the dance as a *métier,* as a technique, as a true profession. Under his influence the stage machinery disappeared. For Petipa, the purpose of ballet was no longer to give ravishing romantic presentations or to sell the erotic appearance of a ballerina but rather to reveal the beauty of the technical mastery of the body. His purpose was often accomplished in an exaggerated manner, but the fact that we now and then feel inclined to speak of his excessive bravura and "circus stunts" should not blind us to the fact that Petipa was the first great master of true dance, perhaps the only one until George Balanchine. Dances (not always entire ballets) choreographed by Petipa are even now a pleasure to observe; the result is an ecstasy of experience that can be aroused only by the art of pure dance. The following descriptions of some of Petipa's ballets are merely an indication (inadequate to be sure) of the master's enormously significant talents. They cannot of course reflect the intense aesthetic emotion derived from witnessing a performance.

It was Petipa primarily who made the development of ballet in Russia possible. Because of him the dance became the most important element of a ballet performance, and the ballerina, through her technique, became the Queen of the Dance.

The Russians occasionally deny Petipa's authorship of, or contributions to, certain ballets. The authorship of a ballet is always a difficult question as we saw in the case of Coralli and Perrot. In general, however, Petipa worked out the choreography in its large outlines. His co-operation with Tchaikovsky was so close that he often prescribed how many measures the great composer should write for one variation or another. The fact that Tchaikovsky could, under such conditions, write music that can be enjoyed, speaks well for the composer. The Russians emphasize Lev Ivanov and regard him—not Petipa—as the choreographer of *The Nutcracker* and also credit him with the principal choreography in *Swan Lake*. D. Leshkov, however, says that the idea for *The Nutcracker* originated with Petipa, who commissioned the music from Tchaikovsky and laid down the number of measures. Because Petipa was incapacitated by illness, Ivanov, an extremely able *maître de ballet,* rehearsed the work, which turned out to be a flat failure. Tchaikovsky was angry, and, according to Leshkov, the press and public believed that Ivanov lacked the inventiveness and creativity necessary for this unusual work.

It was Petipa who gave the *corps de ballet* a clear, almost classic form and who shaped it into a single great instrument, an orchestra. In addition to a trained *corps de ballet,* Petipa's ballets also require fine dancers for the *pas de deux* and the solos.

Petipa did not rely so much on the romantic element as his predecessors had done, nor on the charm of the women; instead, he allowed each of his ballerinas to shine in the light of her own ability and technique.

The technical ability of the male dancer made rapid strides through the teaching of Christian Johannson (1817–1903), pupil of Auguste Bournonville, and Enrico Cecchetti (1850–1928), Italian protégé of Carlo Blasis. Because of the dearth of Russian ballerinas, Italian soloists were sometimes imported, but the Russian women soon assimilated the new ideas rapidly and excelled their Italian colleagues.

Of the male dancers in Moscow, Alexander Gorsky (1876–1924) trained by Platon Karsavin in St. Petersburg, became the most prominent figure. Male dancers in particular owe much to him, for he relied more on the combination of pantomime, mime, and dance than did the St. Petersburg choreographers, and his influence can still be traced in the Bolshoi Ballet today. St. Petersburg remained more *dansant* in its works; and this style was continued by Agrippina Vaganova (1879–1951) even after the Revolution of 1917. For example, just after the Revolution, when it was required in Russia that a ballet had to have something to do with the new ideology, she calmly and successfully revived *Swan Lake.*

In Western Europe during the second half of the nineteenth century, the art of ballet slowly died out. Then a bright star, Adeline Genée, appeared and revitalized it briefly. Genée (born in Denmark in 1878 and trained by her aunt and uncle) was engaged by the Empire Theatre, London, as a ballerina in 1897. Around the turn of the century she was the center of that city's interest in the art of the dance. She retired in 1914 and afterward appeared occasionally only in benefit performances. She was one of the founders of the Camargo Society and the Royal Academy of Dancing.

After 1900 interest in the art of ballet was revived outside of Russia by the Western "invasion" of Russian dancers under the artistic direction of Serge Diaghilev.

BALLETS

Don Quixote

Ballet in a prologue, four acts, eight scenes. Book: Marius Petipa, after Cervantes. Choreography: Marius Petipa. Music: Ludwig Minkus. Première: December 14, 1869, at the Bolshoi Theater, Moscow.

CHARACTERS: Samson Carrasco; Antonina; Don Quixote; Sancho Panza; Lorenzo Corchuelo, an innkeeper; Quiteria (Dulcinea or Aldonza Lorenzo), his daughter; Gamacho; Basilo, a barber; a gypsy chief; Graziosa, his daughter; gypsies; villagers; toreadors; the duke and his retinue; fairies; gnomes; monsters.

PROLOGUE. Don Quixote's study.

Samson Carrasco is wallpapering a bookcase; Antonina is putting an old set of armor into a cupboard. Don Quixote enters reading one of his favorite books. He notices that his bookcase is missing and thinks it has been stolen by evil persons. He sits down and reads attentively tales of knights, combat, and daring deeds. Overcome by weariness, he falls asleep.

Darkness has fallen. Sancho Panza, the servant, comes in through the window with a stolen chicken. A number of angry women are on his heels. Don Quixote wakes up and sends the women away. He then tells Sancho Panza that he is going to become a knight-errant and seek adventure. He takes his helmet and with one blow reduces it to a pile of rusty fragments. Antonina suggests that he would be better off using a basin to protect his head, and Don Quixote follows her advice enthusiastically. Then he looks for armor, a lance, and a shield and prepares for battle.

ACT I. The marketplace in Barcelona.

Quiteria, the innkeeper's daughter, looks out at her lover Basilo. Her father finds her and sends the barber off. Quiteria begins to cry. Now the nobleman Gamacho enters. He, too, is in love with the innkeeper's fair daughter and has come to ask Lorenzo for his daughter's hand. Lorenzo is delighted at the prospect of having such a fine son-in-law.

There is a dance in the marketplace. Toreadors try to embrace the girls, but are prevented from doing so by the girls' lovers. Then Don Quixote riding his horse Rocinante appears, followed by Sancho Panza on a donkey. At his master's command Sancho sounds a blast on the horn. Lorenzo comes out of his inn. Don Quixote thinks that Lorenzo is a nobleman and kneels respectfully. Lorenzo leads Don Quixote to his balcony, while Sancho Panza remains in the marketplace and soon finds himself surrounded by a group of girls who want to play blindman's buff. They take a blanket and toss the servant in it; Don Quixote rushes out to free him. Quiteria appears, and Don Quixote thinks she is a noblewoman bewitched by evil spirits and transported into a different sphere of life. He calls her his Dulcinea. All those present gather again for the dance, while Basilo and Quiteria take the opportunity to slip away. Don Quixote, who has observed their flight, goes after them.

Act II, Scene 1. The inn.

Quiteria and Basilo mingle with people dancing at the inn. At the height of the fun Lorenzo and Gamacho enter and Lorenzo consents to the marriage of Quiteria and Gamacho. Basilo, in despair, reproaches Quiteria for being unfaithful and plunges a dagger into his heart. The dying man then begs Lorenzo to give him his daughter in marriage, but Lorenzo refuses. Fortunately, the knight-errant enters and reproaches Gamacho for not listening to the request of a dying man, but before the two come to blows, the merrymakers drive them from the inn. When Lorenzo consents to the marriage of Quiteria and Basilo, Basilo draws the dagger from his heart. He has played a trick on them and has not really stabbed himself as everyone had believed.

Act II, Scene 2. A gypsy camp near the windmills outside the village.

Graziosa, the daughter of the gypsy leader, is walking with the clown. One of the gypsies announces that the knight-errant is approaching. The chief plans to make a fool of the knight; he puts on a cloak, sets a crown on his head, and sits in state as if he were a king. Don Quixote kneels respectfully before him. At the request of the gypsy chief a show is given for Don Quixote. Several gypsies dance, and a marionette play, featuring a number of soldiers, is presented. Don Quixote thinks that the puppets are live

soldiers, and rushes into combat with them. The gypsies are terrified; Graziosa and the clown leave. Don Quixote emerges victorious
from the fight, and thanks heaven for his victory. Then he thinks
he sees his Dulcinea in the moon. He tries to go to her, but the
windmills block his way so that he can not see her face. He regards
the windmills as giants trying to take Dulcinea from him. With
lance thrust forward, he charges the "giants" but is caught by one
of the arms of a windmill and, after a ride through the air, lands
at the feet of his servant.

ACT III, SCENE 1. A forest.

Sancho Panza enters, walking behind the donkey on which Don
Quixote is sitting. He helps his master off the donkey and onto the
grass. Then he, too, lies down to rest. In his sleep Don Quixote
is troubled by fantastic dreams.

ACT III, SCENE 2. Dulcinea's garden.

A number of fairies, monsters, and gnomes enter, followed by a
horrendous spider spinning its web. Don Quixote attacks the spider
and succeeds in hewing it in two with one stroke. The web falls
apart and reveals the garden of Dulcinea. Don Quixote's beloved
is standing at the entrance surrounded by a group of beautiful girls.

ACT III, SCENE 3. The duke's hunting grounds.

At the sound of a horn, the duke and his retinue appear. Don
Quixote kneels before the duke and is invited to go with him to
the castle.

ACT IV. The duke's castle.

The duke has prepared a feast in honor of Don Quixote, the
Knight of the Doleful Countenance. But Don Quixote's joy is
broken by the Knight of the Silver Moon, who challenges him to
a duel. The Knight of the Doleful Countenance is vanquished and
must promise the Knight of the Moon (who is none other than
Samson Carrasco) to lay aside his sword for a year. The knight-
errant takes off his armor and departs with Sancho Panza.

Several choreographers before Petipa had chosen Don Quixote
as the subject for a ballet: Noverre presented a *Don Quixote*
ballet in Vienna as early as 1750; Louis Milon presented *Les
Noces de Gamache* in Paris in 1801; Paul Taglioni mounted a

ballet on the same subject in Berlin in 1850; and Didelot designed a work in two acts for the dancer Dutacq, with music by
Minkus, in 1865.

Marius Petipa adopted the subject of Don Quixote de la
Mancha, or the Knight of the Doleful Countenance, primarily to
have an opportunity to stage a large number of Spanish dances
and character dances. The human drama and tragedy of Don
Quixote are lost, as the spectator is regaled with a series of brilliant dances and *pas de deux*. Petipa makes the love story of
Quiteria and Basilo the central theme; nonetheless, the spectator
has many solo dances to admire as well as the *Grand Pas de Deux*
(with *pas de deux* double turns) and the *pas d'eventail* (fan
variation). In 1871 Petipa produced a somewhat revised version in St. Petersburg. In 1902 Alexander Gorsky mounted a
revision, with scenery by Konstantin Korovine, which made no
mention of Petipa as author. This setting has remained in repertory, and the Bolshoi Ballet still works with this version.

Anna Pavlova had great success in the role of Quiteria, and,
after she formed her own ballet company in 1914, she took
Petipa's work into repertory, in a shortened version by Laurent
Novikov. Pavlova hired horses for stage appearances during her
tours, but this sometimes caused difficulties. Since most horses
were too well-fed to be convincing as Rocinante, the stage man-
ager doctored up their outward appearance. The metamorphosis
was so realistic that societies for the prevention of cruelty to
animals sometimes protested.

In 1947 Aurel Milloss prepared *Le Portrait de Don Quichotte*
in 1947 for the Ballets des Champs-Elysées, from which version
the American Ballet Theatre took several selections.

Ninette de Valois presented the première of her *Don Quixote*
in Covent Garden on February 20, 1950, with music by Roberto
Gerhard and costumes by Edward Burra. Margot Fonteyn
danced the role of Lady Dulcinea; Robert Helpmann, Don
Quixote; Alexander Grant, Sancho Panza; and the modern
choreographer Kenneth MacMillan, Orlando Furioso. The ballet was presented in five scenes. Some have felt that Ninette de

Valois approached the work too intellectually. In contrast to her predecessors, she followed the subject more closely and used fewer Spanish dance forms.

The *Grand Pas de Deux de Don Quichotte* has been performed by many dancers but its best interpreters have been American and Russian soloists. Lupe Serrano of the American Ballet Theatre was highly acclaimed in the Soviet Union for her dancing of this role. The version usually presented by Western dancers is by Anatole Oboukhoff; in the Soviet Union, by Alexander Gorsky.

Sleeping Beauty

Ballet in a prologue, three acts, five scenes. Book: Marius Petipa and Ivan Vsevolojsky, after tales by Charles Perrault. Choreography: Marius Petipa. Music: P. I. Tchaikovsky. Scenery: Levogt, M. J. Botcharov, Shishkov, and K. M. Ivanov. Costumes: Ivan Vsevolojsky. Première: January 15, 1890, at the Maryinsky Theater, St. Petersburg.

CHARACTERS: king; queen; Princess Aurora, their daughter; Cantalbutte, master of ceremonies; Prince Désiré (sometimes called Prince Florimund); the good fairies; the Lilac Fairy; Carabosse, the wicked fairy; Spanish prince; Italian prince; Indian prince; English prince; Gallison, companion of Prince Désiré; Pierrette; Pierrot; Harlequin; Colombine; Puss-in-Boots; the White Pussy; Cinderella and her prince; the Bluebird and Princess Florissa; Red Riding Hood and the Wolf; four rats; Tom Thumb and his six brothers, with the giant; noblemen; village youths and girls; hunters; nymphs.

PROLOGUE. A spacious hall of a castle, with great columns on both sides. In the foreground, right, a cradle. Left front, a throne. The year: around 1650.

Two nursemaids are watching over the cradle in which the newborn Princess Aurora is asleep. It is her baptismal day. Guests enter, and the master of ceremonies, after approving all the preparations, signals for the king and queen to enter. The royal couple go to the cradle, bend over the child, and kiss her on the cheek. They greet the guests and then take their places on the thrones.

The good fairies arrive and give their blessings to the princess. The most important fairy—the Lilac Fairy—enters last. At a signal from the master of ceremonies, the fairies present their gifts. The presentation takes place in a *pas de six,* in which each fairy performs a solo dance. As they dance, the fairies foretell the future of Princess Aurora. Just as the Lilac Fairy is about to make her prophecy, there is an uproar. A frightened servant enters and reports that the uninvited fairy Carabosse is approaching. She enters the hall in a chariot drawn by four rats; two more rats dressed as men are her pages. With her untidy white dress and wild look, Carabosse is a fearful sight. She is terribly angry that no one invited her to the feast. In any case, she has brought a gift: a golden cage with a rodent in it. Then she makes her evil prophecy: The princess will grow up to be a beautiful girl, but soon after her sixteenth birthday she will prick her finger on a spindle and die from the wound. All are dismayed until the Lilac Fairy comes forward and explains that Princess Aurora will not die, but will sleep until a prince brings her back to life with a kiss. Carabosse gets into her chariot angrily and leaves the castle. The fairies gather round the cradle to protect the baby.

Act I. Sixteen years later. The castle garden.

Village girls and youths bring garlands to adorn the square in front of the castle. A group of spinners come in, laughing and dancing. The master of ceremonies is angry because they have brought their distaffs with them. The king has given orders to conceal any object with points, so that the princess should not prick her finger; otherwise, the prophecy of the wicked Carabosse might come true. Cantalbutte threatens to arrest the women. But before he can do so the king and the queen enter along with four princes vying for Aurora's hand. The crowd acclaims the royal couple. Finally, Princess Aurora enters, radiant and lovely. She greets the Spanish prince and accepts his offering; then she greets the other princes and accepts their offerings in what has become well-known as the Rose Adagio, danced by Aurora and the four suitors. A dance by the girls and young men follows, and is in turn succeeded by variations by Aurora.

Suddenly Aurora sees an old woman with a gleaming object

that she does not recognize. She goes up to the old woman and takes the object in her hand. It is a distaff, and when Aurora touches it she pricks her finger, whirls around helplessly, and falls down. A mocking laugh is heard; the old woman was none other than Carabosse. The four princes draw their daggers, but the witch disappears in flames and smoke as the crowd looks on helplessly. The Lilac Fairy tries to comfort the parents; then, with a wave of her magic wand, she puts everyone to sleep and changes the garden into a dense forest.

ACT II, SCENE 1. The castle, one hundred years later.

Near the castle a hunting party, tired from the hunt, pauses to rest. The group includes Prince Désiré, his faithful companion Gallison, and a number of nobles and ladies. The style of their clothing indicates that a hundred years have elapsed since the first act. One of the ladies begins to annoy Prince Désiré by her attentions. The nobles play blindman's buff as a diversion. Dances by the duchesses, the baronesses, the countesses, and the marquises follow; they end with a farandole and a mazurka, the favorite dances of the nobility at that time.

Horns sound, and the hunt continues. Prince Désiré stays behind, dreaming of a loved one that he has not yet found.

Evening falls. Prince Désiré sees a boat on the lake approaching. It bears the Lilac Fairy. He greets the fairy as she reaches the shore and tells her that he longs for a beautiful princess worthy of his love. The Lilac Fairy magically displays the form of Princess Aurora, and Prince Désiré, impressed by Aurora's beauty entreats the fairy to take him to her. They board the boat and disappear in the distance.

ACT II, SCENE 2. The hall of the enchanted castle.

In the middle of the hall is a bed, on which Princess Aurora lies in a deep slumber. The prince and the fairy enter. The prince is enchanted by the sleeping princess. He bends over and kisses her. Aurora awakens, sits up, and the prince takes her in his arms. After a hundred years the spell of the wicked fairy Carabosse is broken.

ACT III. The great hall of the castle.

The others in the castle also awaken; life begins again. The master of ceremonies, who supervises everything, bustles about preparing for a celebration. The king and the queen arrive to preside over the betrothal ceremonies. The guests dance a polonaise, which is followed by a series of *divertissements*. Harlequin, Colombine, Pierrot, and Pierrette dance a *pas de quatre*. Puss-in-Boots and the White Pussy appear in a character dance, followed by a *pas de quatre* by Cinderella and her prince with the Bluebird and Princess Florissa. A character dance by Little Red Riding Hood and the Wolf is followed by another dance by Cinderella and her prince. Finally, Tom Thumb appears with his brothers and the giant. After all the guests have danced, it is the turn of Princess Aurora and Prince Désiré. They dance the famous *Grand Pas de Deux*. The entire company then performs a saraband and, for the finale, a mazurka. The good fairies gather around the happy pair. Good has overcome evil.

The Sleeping Beauty is a typical nineteenth-century production, a fairy-tale ballet in which it is not the story that counts but the opportunity for variations and solos which may or may not have a logical connection with the subject matter. This well-loved work lasts an entire evening in its full-length version and is so expensive to stage that usually only government-supported ensembles can afford to take it into their repertories.

Alexandre Benois, the well-known Russian painter and art critic, has written a full description of the première in *Reminiscences of the Russian Ballet*. He considered both the production as a whole and the music splendid, but criticized the costumes as amateurish and lacking in poetic spirit. According to Benois, Petipa outdid himself in the choreography, particularly in the various dances of the fairies in the Prologue, the *Grand Pas de Deux*, the Bluebird *pas de deux*, the saraband, and the mazurka —all of which he regarded as masterpieces. Paul Gerdt as Prince Désiré and Carlotta Brianza as Aurora were, for Benois, ideal interpreters, and he was also impressed by Enrico Cecchetti, who danced both the pantomime role of the evil fairy Carabosse and the part of the Bluebird. Stukolkin, as the master of ceremonies, held his own with Gerdt. The work as a whole, wrote Benois, had a typically Russian atmosphere, despite the foreign influences, but the choreography by the Frenchman Petipa, the principal roles played by Italian dancers, and the music by Tchaikovsky reflected Western influences. Although the color of the costumes did not meet with his approval, nonetheless, he felt that Vsevolojsky made a great contribution to the atmosphere of the ballet by having it played in two different periods and adhering to the costumes of each.

The work has also been returned to the repertoire in Russia. Konstantin Sergeyev mounted a version for the Leningrad Kirov Ballet, following the Petipa choreography as closely as possible. In 1944 the Bolshoi Ballet presented a production by Asaf Messerer and designs by Isaac Rabinovitch.

The Ballets Russes of Serge Diaghilev staged a short revival (three months) of *The Sleeping Beauty* at the Alhambra Theatre, London, on November 2, 1921. Nicholas Sergeyev was in charge of rehearsals and based the choreography on oral traditions of dancers from the Imperial Russian Ballet and on his own recollections. Léon Bakst designed the scenery and costumes. Several changes were made in this version—for example, Stravinsky's new compositions of the Prelude to the third scene and the variation for Aurora in that scene. The dance of the hunters and Aurora's variation in the third scene were staged by Bronislava Nijinska. The dance of Cinderella and her prince and the dance by Tom Thumb, his brothers, and the giant were replaced by two Oriental dances from *The Nutcracker*—the *danse arabe* and the *danse chinoise*. The *Danse de la Fée Dragée* by the Lilac Fairy in the Prologue was also taken from *The Nutcracker*. Further additions were the variation of Bluebeard and his wives and the dance of Innocent Ivan and his brothers. Many prominent dancers participated in the Diaghilev revival: Vera Trefilova, Lubov Egorova, Lydia Lopokova, and Olga Spessivtzeva alternated in the role of Princess Aurora; Pierre Vladimiroff danced Prince Désiré, and Stanislas Idzikovsky, the Bluebird. Lopokova and Bronislava Nijinska shared the role of the Lilac Fairy. Carlotta Brianza, the original Aurora, danced Carabosse in the revival; later in the season, Enrico Cecchetti danced the role—one which he had created in the original Maryinsky production—to celebrate his fiftieth year as a performer.

The Sadler's Wells Ballet first produced the work on February 2, 1939. Nicholas Sergeyev was also in charge of this production. Margot Fonteyn danced Princess Aurora, and Robert Helpmann was the Prince. The settings were not very successful, and new sets and costumes were provided by Oliver Messel in 1956.

In 1955 the Berlin Opera produced the ballet under the supervision of Tatiana Gsovsky. Germany has also seen a short version of the work produced by Hans Zehden with music by Hans Werner after Tchaikovsky.

In America various companies have presented Act III of the work under the title *Aurora's Wedding* (Original Ballet Russe, Ballet Russe de Monte Carlo) or *Princess Aurora* (Ballet Theatre).

On October 27, 1960, the Marquis de Cuevas Ballet presented the *Sleeping Beauty* at the Théâtre des Champs-Elysées, Paris. Bronislava Nijinska rehearsed the production, and afterwards Robert Helpmann took it over. Rosella Hightower and Nina Vyroubova alternated in the role of Aurora. This full-length ballet was the swan song of the Marquis de Cuevas, who died on February 22, 1961, at Cannes.

The Nutcracker ("Casse Noisette")

Ballet in two acts, three scenes. Book: Marius Petipa. Choreography: begun by Marius Petipa, completed by Lev Ivanov. Music: P. I. Tschaikovsky. Sets and costumes: M. J. Botcharov and K. M. Ivanov. Première: December 17, 1892, at the Maryinsky Theater, St. Petersburg.

CHARACTERS: the governor; his wife; their children Franz and Clara; Uncle Drosselmeyer; Aunt Marianna; governess; servants; mechanical dolls; canteen woman; soldier; Columbine; Harlequin; King of the Mice; Nutcracker; Sugarplum Fairy; Prince Koklush; children; guests; fairies; mice; snowflakes; biscuits; the Merveilleuse; incroyables.

❧

Act I, Scene 1.

It is Christmas Eve and the governor and his wife are giving a party for their children, Clara and Franz. The guests arrive, and the children and their parents dance. The clock strikes nine and Uncle Drosselmeyer, apparently one of the most welcome guests, enters. He has brought four mechanical dolls with him as a present; these do a *pas de quatre*. When the time comes for the children to go to bed, Uncle Drosselmeyer pulls one more surprise out of his bag for Clara: a pretty nutcracker. Franz is jealous of the nutcracker, and there is a squabble. Franz breaks the nutcracker, and Clara bursts into tears. She stops crying when the uncle bandages the broken toy and asks her to put it to bed. The grown-ups perform the so-called Grandfather dance, ending the party. Everyone leaves.

The room is dark; only the Christmas tree with its lights can be seen. Clara lies in bed but can not fall asleep, for she is thinking of the nutcracker. She climbs out of bed to look at it. As she approaches the tree, she sees a wondrous thing. The mended Nutcracker is leading a company of soldiers in battle against a horde of mice directed by the nine-headed King of the Mice. Clara does not hesitate to take the side of Nutcracker, and through her assistance Nutcracker defeats the mice. Nutcracker then changes into a handsome young man, and he invites Clara to go with him to the land of sweets.

Act I, Scene 2.

Clara and the young man, making their way to the land of sweets, journey through a cold country swept by snow and hail. The Snow King and Queen order the snowflakes to lie down, and they themselves pay homage to Clara and the Nutcracker-youth in a *pas de deux;* they wish the pair a good trip.

Act II.

Clara and the Nutcracker arrive in the land of sweets, where a candy house melts under the rays of the sun. The Sugarplum Fairy welcomes them and organizes a festival for their entertainment. A series of character dances follow, and finally there is a *pas de deux* by the Sugarplum Fairy and the Prince. Everyone takes part in the finale. The ballet ends with an *apotheosis:* Bees busy gathering honey dance around the hive and bring tribute to the Queen.

❧

Marius Petipa, who was choreographer and ballet master at the Maryinsky Theater from 1862–1903, asked Tchaikovsky to compose the music for *The Nutcracker* (a ballet based on E. T. A. Hoffmann's *The Nutcracker and the King of the Mice*). The composer was at first not greatly attracted to the idea, but his interest gradually increased, and he began to compose the music in 1891, finishing it in July of that year. Petipa had sketched the ballet in large outline, but illness prevented him from conducting the rehearsals, so Lev Ivanov, his assistant, substituted for him.

At the première Antoinetta Dell'Era danced the role of the Sugarplum Fairy; Nicholas Legat, Nutcracker; and Paul Gerdt, Prince Koklush. Although the work was warmly applauded, it was some time before it was accepted by both the public and the press. In the end, *The Nutcracker* won its permanent place in repertory.

Since the première, various changes have been made in the ballet, and each new production has introduced further alterations so that now it is difficult to say what the "authentic" setting should be. For example, the Nutcracker sometimes turns into a handsome young man in the first scene, but there are also versions in which his transformation does not take place until the second scene. The character dances of Act II are usually designed anew by the choreographer or *maître de ballet* staging the work. The Arabian dance is often a far cry from the stomach dance of the Orient; and the Chinese dance also frequently leaves much to be desired.

Nicholas Sergeyev staged the first Western production of the work for the Sadler's Wells Ballet, presented in 1934, with Alicia Markova and Harold Turner. It has been revived from time to time in England, where for some years it has also been the custom to present the Act II *pas de deux* at Christmas time.

Some fine productions have been staged: the Ballet Russe de Monte Carlo production in 1940, choreographed by Alexander Fedorova "after Petipa," with Alicia Markova and André Eglevsky; the London Festival version in 1950, rehearsed by Nicholas Beriosov, with Alicia Markova and Anton Dolin; and the Frederick Ashton revision (1951) for Sadler's Wells Theatre Ballet, with Elaine Fifield and David Blair.

In 1954 the New York City Ballet revived the complete ballet with choreography by George Balanchine. Maria Tallchief danced the Sugarplum Fairy and Nicholas Magallanes, the Prince. (André Eglevsky, scheduled to appear, was prevented from doing so because of an ankle injury.) Since then, *The Nutcracker* has been successfully presented every Christmas season, a delightful tradition for spectators—mostly children. As far as content and subject matter are concerned, this ballet lends itself better to performances for children than for adults, since only Act II can pretend to the name "ballet." Children, incidentally, are the principal participants in this production; professional dancers appear primarily in the various *divertissements* in the second act. In 1958 the New York City Ballet's version of *The Nutcracker* was televised. At this performance the role of the old, comic uncle was interpreted by George Balanchine, the leading partisan of the "music ballet," though few of the viewers recognized him.

Swan Lake ("Le Lac des Cygnes")

Ballet in four acts. Book: V. P. Begitchev and Vasily Geltzer. Choreography: Marius Petipa and Lev Ivanov. Music: P. I. Tchaikovsky. Première: January 27, 1895, at the Maryinsky Theater, St. Petersburg.

CHARACTERS: Prince Siegfried; his mother; Wolfgang, the prince's tutor; Benno, a friend of the prince; Odette; Von Rotbart, an evil genius; Odile, his daughter; hunters; country girls and youths; retinue of Siegfried's mother; cygnets; swans; guests; jester; pages.

❧

ACT I. A garden with a castle in the background.

A feast to celebrate the coming of age of Prince Siegfried is in progress. Country girls and young men arrive to congratulate the prince. Siegfried's friend Benno dances with two charming girls and the court jester moves around among the guests. Siegfried's mother enters with her retinue. She is not at all pleased with the company Siegfried keeps and reminds him that it is time for him to choose a bride; his choice must be made at the ball on the following day. Then she leaves, followed by her suite. The young people continue their merrymaking. Siegfried's tutor, who has drunk a little too much, criticizes the dancing and tries to demonstrate the old-style dance with one of the girls. Everybody laughs at him. The jester begins to play the fool and goes through all kinds of acrobatics. Festivities are at their height. Benno dances again with the two beauties. Finally, most of the dancers divide into pairs and leave the garden in a snake dance. The tutor, Siegfried, and Benno watch them go. A flight of swans passes overhead, and Siegfried and his friend impulsively decide to go swan hunting. The jester is instructed to keep the tutor behind so that Siegfried can be free at least once. All leave the garden.

ACT II. A clearing in the forest, with a lake in the background. In the distance, a ruin; to the right, a rock. Shortly before midnight.

A flock of swans comes gliding over the lake. The swans are bewitched maidens in the power of the evil genius Von Rotbart; they take on human form only from midnight until daybreak. In the forefront swims a swan with a coronet on her head. Von Rotbart, who always keeps a watchful eye on his swan-maidens, sends back the first four swans that arrive, then sits down on a rock. Siegfried enters and suddenly finds himself surrounded by a group of girls, who, after dancing around for a few moments, disappear and make room for Odette, their leader. Odette cries out upon seeing the prince. Siegfried goes over to her, picks her up and whirls her around. The evil genius, who looks somewhat like an ugly bird with great wings, leaps between Odette and Siegfried and drives Siegfried off. A short dance by Odette and Von Rotbart follows. Then both leave as the *corps de ballet* enters in a long line.

The prince returns again, and Odette, who seems to have escaped the evil spirit for the moment, reappears. Some variations follow, including a *pas de trois* by three swans. Then Odette and Siegfried, who evidently have been strolling through the woods, return to dance a *pas de deux*, which is followed by a pretty solo for Odette. The prince does not dance much by himself; he is too absorbed in admiring Odette. Then a *pas de quatre* by four young swans (the popular "cygnet" number) and a *pas de trois* by three larger swans take place. Siegfried now tells Odette in a *pas de deux* that he loves her and that he has decided to choose her for his wife; he invites her to come to his birthday ball, where he will present her as his betrothed. Odette replies that she can not come to the ball until the power of Von Rotbart is broken; she tells the prince that Von Rotbart will leave no stone unturned to keep them apart. If the prince breaks his marriage vow, she and her friends must die; if he lives up to his pledge, she can retain human form forever.

A shimmer of light announces the coming of day. The girls leave, and the swans glide away over the lake. Siegfried remains. Odette returns to say goodbye again. The evil spirit flaps his wings in warning. Odette must go. Siegfried stretches his arms out to her, but Odette takes flight.

ACT III. A magnificent ballroom. To the right, a throne; to the left, a staircase.

A master of ceremonies ushers in the guests. All await the coming of Siegfried and his mother. The queen comes down the staircase with her retinue and, after the usual greetings, takes her place on the throne. The court jester entertains the company with a solo. All form in pairs for the dance. Siegfried enters and seems greatly preoccupied. The company take their places along the sides of the ballroom. Four masked pairs dance. Then the girls, from among whom Siegfried is expected to choose his bride, dance in turn, but none knows that Siegfried has already made his choice and that she is not among these lovely ladies. Guests from distant lands execute some of their national dances: a Neapolitan dance, a mazurka, and a Hungarian dance. Siegfried, bemused, dances with some of the debutantes. Where is Odette? The queen tries to persuade her son to make his choice known, but Siegfried refuses. The court jester announces some belated guests. They are Von Rotbart and his daughter Odile, whom he has made into the image of Odette. Odile is dressed not in white, but in black. Odile withdraws with Siegfried while the Spanish couples, who entered with Von Rotbart, do a Spanish dance. Von Rotbart, confident that his plan will succeed, takes a place next to the queen as if it belonged to him. Odile returns and dances a solo. The prince looks on, enthralled; Odile never looks at Von Rotbart. In high spirits, Siegfried executes a solo and then the pair perform the well-known "Black Swan" *pas de deux*. At its conclusion, Siegfried tells the company that his choice is made: Odette shall be his wife. The queen takes the pseudo-Odette by the arm and presents her to the guests. Then the real Odette appears, amidst thunder and lightning, in the background behind the big window in the ballroom. Siegfried is frightened. Von Rotbart laughs devilishly and runs away with his daughter. The queen vanishes, and Siegfried leaves. There is general confusion on stage.

ACT IV. Once again the forest clearing near the lake. The rock of Act II now replaced by a crumbling castle.

The swan maidens dance while waiting for Odette to return from the castle. The queen enters, dejected; Sigfried, she tells them, has broken his promise. A clap of thunder announces the arrival of Von Rotbart, and the swan-maidens depart. There is a short dance by Von Rotbart and Odette, in which Von Rotbart rejoices that he still has her in his power. At the end of the dance, the magician lays Odette on the ground where Siegfried finds her. The swan-maidens return and listen as Siegfried tries to convince Odette of his true love; Odette forgives him. Flashes of lightning shoot through the sky. The swan-maidens are afraid. Von Rotbart enters again and makes a final effort to retain his power. Odette believes all is lost and flees to the lake. Siegfried catches her before she plunges in, although Von Rotbart tries to prevent him. Siegfried then cuts off one of the magician's wings. Odette's friends become more and more fearful. Lightning continues to kindle the night sky. The old castle collapses with a roar and finally Von Rotbart falls. Siegfried's love is stronger than the evil of the magician.

The light grows stronger; the sun rises; Siegfried and Odette are saved. Siegfried kneels at the feet of his beloved Odette. The swan-maidens, liberated from Von Rotbart's power, may keep their human shape. They crowd around the happy pair.

❧

The version described above is that of the Bolshoi Ballet, choreographed by Alexander Gorsky (Acts I, II, and III) and Asaf Messerer (Act IV).

Most of the versions of the ballet are said to be based upon Petipa. Actually no two productions have the same steps, figures, and staging; and "authenticity" is an unknown concept. As presented on the Western stage, Act II brings Siegfried's friends on stage at the beginning, armed with bows and arrows to hunt the swans. When the friends see the swans in the air, they tell Siegfried. As the hunters are about to shoot the birds, Siegfried waves them away. Odette reveals herself to Siegfried in human form. Siegfried and Odette leave the stage, which becomes filled with the white swans. Benno's friends enter, rejoicing that the birds are within range. Siegfried returns just in time to prevent the shooting and inform the hunters that these are no swans, but bewitched maidens! (The modern Russian version of the entire ballet is a bit more believable, although it too has some aspects of the staging that do not make much sense.)

In 1877 Julius Reisinger presented *Swan Lake*, with music by Tchaikovsky, at the Bolshoi Theater, Moscow. The ballet was a complete failure, and Tchaikovsky attributed its lack of success to his music—which he proposed to revise. However, the composer died before undertaking the project. Petipa thought that the composition was thoroughly usable, and he completed the second act in 1894. The entire *Swan Lake* was presented in 1895, in honor of the ballerina Pierina Legnani, who danced Odette; Paul Gerdt was the prince.

There are still some differences of opinion whether Petipa or Ivanov should be credited with the choreography in *Swan Lake*. Petipa made rather detailed sketches and left the production to Ivanov, but it is not clear how the work was divided. Some critics believe that Petipa was the creator of the first three acts, and Ivanov of the fourth act. Others maintain that Ivanov was responsible for Act II and Act IV—the so-called white acts because of the classical, white dress of the *corps de ballet*.

In 1901 Alexander Gorsky mounted a new version for the Imperial Ballet at Moscow. Later the fourth act was redone by Asaf Messerer.

Swan Lake was first given in a complete version in England by the Sadler's Wells Ballet at the Sadler's Wells Theatre, London, in 1934 with the Petipa-Ivanov choreography created by Nicholas Sergeyev; Alicia Markova and Robert Helpmann danced the principal roles. There have been subsequent Sadler's Wells productions in 1943, 1948, and 1952. For the Sadler's Wells production in 1952 Frederick Ashton created a *pas de six* for the first act and a Neopolitan dance for the third act.

The roles of Odette-Odile, originally conceived for two dancers, are usually danced by one ballerina. Some famous interpreters of Odette-Odile have been Anna Pavlova, Thamar Karsavina, Olga Preobrajenska, Mathilde Kchesinska, Alica Markova, Alexandra Danilova, and Margot Fonteyn. Prince Siegfried has received fine interpretations by Serge Lifar, Vaslav Nijinsky, Mikhail Mordkin, and others. The famous ballerina Rosella Hightower made her name in the "Black Swan" section danced with André Eglevsky.

The second act frequently appears independently of the others in ballet repertories and is known as a *ballet blanc* (a ballet containing more dance than pantomime, and in which the women wear white tutus).

George Balanchine revamped Act II of *Swan Lake* after the St. Petersburg version. The première of his production took place on November 20, 1951, at the New York City Center, with Maria Tallchief and André Eglevsky. Cecil Beaton designed the scenery and costumes. The choreography is beautiful, but there has been a good deal of controversy about the authenticity of the steps and figures. Balanchine himself stated that only the central *adagio* and the *pas de quatre* of the cygnets of the original remained. However, since the première, he has continued to revise the choreography and now only the cygnets' *pas de quatre* is left.

Since Petipa always subordinated the male dancer, the present-day Bolshoi version by Vladimir Bourmeister (who follows the same policy), with supplementary music by Tchaikovsky, gives the impression of being more authentic than most Western versions. In this interpretation (première on April 25, 1953) the prince has a very small dancing role, although the Russians certainly have no lack of good *danseurs*. The staging of the Bolshoi Ballet is worked out logically and carefully.

The first performance in America was given at the Metropolitan Opera House in 1911, with Catherine Geltzer. Mikhail Mordkin presented his company in *Swan Lake* in 1937.

Les Sylphides

Ballet in one act, seven parts. Choreography: Michel Fokine. Music: Frederic Chopin. Scenery: Alexandre Benois. Première: June 2, 1909, at the Théâtre du Châtelet, Paris, by the Serge Diaghilev Company.

PRINCIPALS: three female soloists, one male soloist, and an all-female *corps de ballet*.

As the curtain rises, following the overture, the dancers are seen grouped against the backdrop—a moonlit forest with a ruined castle. The ensemble dance the nocturne. One of the soloists executes the waltz; then another soloist dances the mazurka. The second mazurka is a solo for the *danseur*. The prelude, once more repeated, is danced by the third female soloist, who then dances the waltz, a *pas de deux* with the male soloist; this is the high point of the ballet. The *corps de ballet* stands in groups on the stage and changes its position slightly from time to time. The *corps de ballet* presents the great waltz; at its climax the soloists appear on stage again. At the decrescendo there is a return to the original grouping, and as the curtain falls, the entire ensemble is in the same position as at the outset. It is as if a dream had briefly come to life.

❧

Les Sylphides is a difficult ballet to perform well. At least three elements of a performance are critical for achievement of the desired tone and atmosphere: the *port de bras* of the dancers, the lighting of the stage, and the musical tempi.

The ballet seems to have suggested itself to Fokine after he heard Alexander Glazunov's orchestration of four of Chopin's compositions: a polonaise, a nocturne, a mazurka, and a tarantella. At Fokine's request Glazunov inserted an orchestration of a Chopin waltz.

Three versions preceded the one commonly known as *Les Sylphides*. The first version, choreographed by Fokine and entitled *Chopiniana,* was given at a benefit performance in St. Petersburg in 1907. The polonaise was danced in Polish costumes in a ballroom setting. For the nocturne, Fokine drew his inspiration from a legendary incident in Chopin's life: The ghost of a monk interrupts Chopin who is composing at a piano, but the composer's Muse appears and drives the menacing figure off, so that the creative work can be resumed. The Polish wedding served as the theme for the mazurka, which celebrates the approaching marriage between a young girl and an elderly man. The waltz was a classic *pas de deux* danced on this occasion by Anatole Oboukhoff and Anna Pavlova, the latter wearing a long white tutu reminiscent of the sylph's costume in *La Sylphide*. (This dance, incidentally, gave the first indication of the form into which *Les Sylphides* finally evolved.) Finally, the tarentella was performed by an ensemble, with children added to make the scene more lifelike; the setting represented the city of Naples, with Vesuvius in the background.

In 1908 the second version of this ballet was used at a benefit performance in the Maryinsky Theater, St. Petersburg. The ballet had been thoroughly revised as a *ballet blanc*. The soloists were Olga Preobrajenska, Anna Pavlova, Thamar Karsavina, and Vaslav Nijinsky—no less!

Also in 1908 a third version was given, using new costumes

and an orchestration by Maurice Keller (the Grande Valse was contributed by Glazunov), for a student audience. (Later, the orchestration was supplied by others including Anatole Liadov, Nicholas Tcherepnin, Igor Stravinsky, and even the various conductors.) Diaghilev chose this work for his West European repertory, and in 1909 the ballet was given in Paris with Thamar Karsavina, Anna Pavlova, Maria Baldina, and Vaslav Nijinsky as soloists, and with no important choreographic changes. But the title was changed to *Les Sylphides,* on the advice of the painter Alexandre Benois, who thought the new name would cause people to associate the ballet with the romantic story of *La Sylphide.*

Les Sylphides is generally regarded both as a typically romantic ballet and as a typical Diaghilev ballet. This view is only partly true. Romantic it does seem to be. From the mazurka on, it has a dream-like atmosphere; the ballerinas are enveloped in a cloud of tulle; and the music of Chopin and the settings are purely romantic. Is it any wonder that the name "sylphides," spirits of the air, was given to the dancers? It will be seen in the next chapter, however, that *Les Sylphides* is not a typical Diaghilev ballet; indeed it should not be considered a Diaghilev ballet at all, inasmuch as it was choreographed before the Diaghilev ballet group was formed.

Les Sylphides may be regarded as a new art form, in that it represented a transition from the unreality of Romanticism to the modern "abstract" or symphonic or music ballet, in which, according to Dr. Hornstra, "dance movements arranged rhythmically in time and phrased melodically in space" finally achieve a life of their own and lead to the art of the dance proper. It is not hard to place *Les Sylphides*: It has the same place in ballet art as Debussy has in music.

It is also Fokine's masterpiece. It came in a period when the choreographer was not yet completely submerged by Bakst and Benois, by the set and costume designers, and by Diaghilev, the art organizer and businessman. (For this reason it is grouped here with other works created during the period of Russian ascendancy, instead of being placed in the Diaghilev period.)

Fokine staged *Les Sylphides* in 1925 for the Royal Danish Ballet; he revived the ballet again in 1936 for René Blum's Ballets de Monte Carlo, changing the solo part of the male dancer (to the detriment of the work, says the Englishman, Cyril Beaumont). In 1940 he also staged a version for the American Ballet Theatre. Indeed, since its first performance in Paris, the ballet has entered the repertory of most large companies, where it still remains.

A number of designers have provided sets for this work. It has even been performed in a setting from the opera *Ivan the Terrible*. Léon Zack, Eugene Dunkel, A. Socrate, and countless others created settings for *Les Sylphides*. Carzou, a modern French designer, prepared sets for the Paris Opéra some years ago, but they were unfortunately inappropriate. His forest, like a wilderness that would never come to life, suggested the atomic age, and the sets have now been stored in the depository of the Opéra.

5

Diaghilev: The Russian Ballet In Western Europe

Interest in the ballet was at a low point in western Europe around the turn of the century. Leo Staats (1877–1952) a disciple of Louis Mérante, arranged dances for the Opéra and for musicals, but his contributions did not bring much that was really new.

Then, suddenly in 1900, Isadora Duncan (1878–1927) arrived in Paris from the United States and immediately attracted an enthusiastic following. She represented young America, resentful of Puritanism and the narrow ideas of Old and New England, and ready to use spiritual weapons borrowed from Old Europe to achieve a new freedom. The message she brought was one of revolt—against anything that restricted the "natural" development of the body. She traveled to many European cities and in 1905 appeared in St. Petersburg, where Fokine soon became one of her many admirers. She was a truly remarkable personality. Seeking to return to the culture of ancient Greece, she studied Greek vase painting and wore a transparent tunic instead of satin slippers and tights. She danced to music by Gluck,

Mozart, Beethoven, and Schubert, but her art of the dance was not such that a school could be derived from it. Neither did she belong to the art of ballet. As a matter of fact, her dancing was directed primarily against the shackles of ballet. But her message was contemporary in Europe with the revolt against excess artificiality, a movement to which she gave new impetus. Although she vaguely anticipated the expressionism of the twenties, her roots were clearly in the prewar world.

It is not difficult to understand why Isadora Duncan made an impression on the young Russian choreographer, Fokine, then only twenty-five years old. Away with the bodice of the rigid ballet; overboard with silly fables that have nothing to do with the feelings and desires of human beings; banish fantasies and fancies and replace them with direct feelings and simple actions. Although Fokine remained true to ballet, the influence was evident in his efforts to use simple means to depict feelings and sentiments with a great deal of atmosphere and lighting effects, but without much action. In 1905, the year he first saw Isadora Duncan, Fokine created *The Dying Swan,* which Anna Pavlova later made famous on her tours throughout the world. And after *Eunice* (a typical Duncan ballet) he created the mature ballet *Les Sylphides* (1909), an enduring masterpiece. Unfortunately, Fokine's development ended there, for he was thereafter influenced mainly by the impresario Diaghilev, the organizer and giver of commissions.

Serge Diaghilev (1872–1929) originally went to St. Petersburg to study law, but his interest in art proved to be greater than his interest in law. He soon organized intimate evening concerts, attended the ballet and opera regularly, and became interested in painting. In 1898, with the financial support of Princess Tenishev and the manufacturer Sava Momontov, he founded an art magazine which lasted until 1904. In 1900 Prince Serge Volkonsky of the Imperial Theater commissioned him to do the Theater Yearbook, but the commission was withdrawn the next year, following a quarrel. A few years later Diaghilev began to organize art exhibitions in collaboration with Benois. The first exhibition in 1905 was unsuccessful because of the war between Russia and Japan. Subsequently Diaghilev decided to teach the West about Russian art, and in 1906 he organized an exhibition of Russian painting in Paris, followed in 1907 by a number of concerts at the Opéra, and in 1908 by the opera *Boris Godunov,* in which Parisians first heard the famous bass Fyodor Chaliapin.

Encouraged by success, Diaghilev presented several Russian ballets in Paris in 1909. He organized and directed the enterprise with the assistance of the painters Léon Bakst and Benois. Other collaborators were N. Tcherepnin, a young friend and composer; Valerian Svetlov, the ballet critic; and the youthful Fokine.

The opening night marking the beginning of Diaghilev's first period took place at the Théâtre du Châtelet on May 19, 1909. It was an event that people were to talk about for decades. The program included dances from *Prince Igor* (to music by Borodin, with the ballerinas Elena Smirnova and Sophie Fedorova and the male dancer Adolph Bolm) and Benois' beloved ballet *Le Pavilion d'Armide* (to music by N. Tcherepnin, with the ballerinas Thamar Karsavina and Vera Karalli and the *danseurs* Vaslav Nijinsky and Mikhail Mordkin). Although the ballet *Cleopatre* was not yet ready for production, a *divertissement* of dances from it was also given—under the title *Le Festin.* The first performance was followed by many more which included, among others, the following ballets choreographed by Michel Fokine: *Les Sylphides* (1909), *Cleopatre* (1909), *Carnaval* (1910), *Scheherazade* (1910), *The Firebird* (1910), *Le Spectre de la Rose* (1911), *Petrouchka* (1911), *Thamar* (1912), and *Le Coq d'Or* (1914).

The performance on May 29, 1912, of *L'Après-midi d'un Faune,* choreographed and danced by Vaslav Nijinsky, caused a great scandal because many considered the work immoral. *Le Sacre du Printemps* (May 29, 1913), also Nijinsky's ballet, was a memorable event because of the then sensational music of Igor Stravinsky.

The spectators at all these ballets came in droves from many countries of Europe, and were dazzled by the barbaric riot of color. Their ears became attuned to the rich melodies of the Russian composers Mussorgsky, Rimsky-Korsakov, Glazunov, and Tcherepnin. Then Stravinsky made his debut in western Europe with sounds and dissonances never before heard; audiences were bewildered by the strange music. And, too, they were amazed by the superior technique of the dancers and overwhelmed by an avalanche of stars. Thamar Karsavina, Anna Pavlova, Catherine Geltzer, Mathilde Kchesinska, Vaslav Nijinsky, Adolph Bolm, Paul Gerdt, and Mikhail Mordkin surpassed anything that had been seen up to that time.

The first period of Diaghilev's career was especially spectacular, mainly because of the colorful staging and extraordinary music. Fokine had won renown as a choreographer, but we would hesitate to rank the highly promising choreographer of *Les Sylphides* among the great ones of choreography. Indeed, his dances were subordinate, mere adjuncts, to the opulent colors of scenery and costumes. It was the music that primarily enchanted the audiences. In addition, the décors and costumes attracted a large share of the spectators' attention, as did the soloists' techniques, which impressed the West as simply fabulous. Diaghilev worked principally with soloists, as had been the custom in nineteenth-century ballet. The *corps de ballet* was excellent, it is true; but Fokine could do nothing with a *corps* enveloped in long, often heavy clothing that was sometimes fur-trimmed! In contrast to the richly ornamented, overburdened corps, the soloists in their short tutus or tight *maillots* could show their powers brilliantly. Fokine sometimes created a "confusion of steps," an intricately worked out dance pattern for the *corps de ballet* (as in *Petrouchka*); sometimes he was content to introduce, practically intact, Russian folk dances; but most often he treated the *corps* very statically (as in *The Firebird*). Fokine certainly managed this static *corps de ballet* well, but he was caught midway between the new and the old; he introduced nothing particularly novel in the art of ballet, nor could he be considered an effective guardian of established traditions. As noted in the preceding chapter, his works represented mainly a transition period between the romantic ballet and the modern abstract ballet.

With the departure of Michel Fokine in 1914, Diaghilev's first period came to an end. Fokine returned to Russia and eventually settled in the United States in 1923. Anna Pavlova also left Diaghilev's company. She and Diaghilev were too imperious to work well together, and in 1914 she formed a company of her own. As a ballerina she introduced little that was new to the art of the dance, but through her the whole world became acquainted with ballet dancing. Indeed we might characterize her as "an ambassadress for the ballet." Nijinsky, Diaghilev's favorite dancer, married Romola de Pulsky in South America in 1913 and was summarily dismissed from the company by Diaghilev as soon as he had word of the marriage. Shortly thereafter Nijinsky was found to be suffering from schizophrenia, and he was in and out of asylums until his death in 1950.

The departure of Fokine, Pavlova, and Nijinsky thinned the ranks, and something had to be done to give the company renewed impetus. Diaghilev searched in Russia for a replacement for Fokine and finally chose Léonide Massine (1894–   ).

Diaghilev's second period began with Massine and was marked by works that are less typically Russian. Massine became prominent as a choreographer around 1915. Airy and *dansant* in his constructions, he always liked a joke—provided that the laugh was on his side. He has stated that he prefers to design abstract rather than realistic ballets, but his attempts to do this have not shown him at his best. Massine designed, among others, *Les Femmes de Bonne Humeur* (1917), with music by D. Scarlatti and scenery by Léon Bakst; *La Boutique Fantasque* (1919); and *The Three-Cornered Hat* (*Le Tricorne*, 1919).

Nijinsky's sister, Bronislava Nijinska (1890–   ), came to the fore as a choreographer with *Les Noces* (1923), to music by Igor Stravinsky, with scenery and costumes by Nathalie Gontcharova; *Les Biches* (1924), to music by Francis Poulenc, and with scenery and curtain by Marie Laurencin; *Le Train Bleu* (1924), to music by Darius Milhaud, and with costumes by Chanel, scenery by Laurens, and a curtain by Picasso; and a number of other ballets. Though she never created great works, she consistently demonstrated exceptional skill, justifying her reputation as a competent professional.

(It may be noted in passing that in 1923 the principality of Monaco engaged Diaghilev's company as the official ballet of its opera company; his ballet group was subsequently named the Ballets Russes de Monte Carlo.)

The third period of Diaghilev's work, from 1925 to 1929, was highlighted by the contributions of the choreographer George Balanchine (1904–   ). Balanchine, who made his debut in western Europe, developed into a worthy follower of Marius Petipa and became the foremost choreographer of our time. He created *La Pastorale* to music by Georges Auric, with scenery by Pruna (1926); *Le Triomphe de Neptune* to music by Lord Berners (1926); *La Chatte* to music by Henri Sauguet, with scenery by Gabo and Pevsner (1927); *Apollon Musagète* to music by Igor Stravinsky, with scenery by André Bauchant (1928); *Le Fils Prodigue* (1929); and a number of other works. Massine and Bronislava Nijinska were still working with Diaghilev in this period, and the Russian dancer Serge Lifar also designed one of the ballets. But the typically Russian atmosphere gave way to one more marked by West European influence. Nathalie Gontcharova and her husband, Michael Larionov, still represented the old Russia, although they were strongly influenced by *Jugendstil-Art Nouveau*. Picasso, Rouault, Derain, and others were representatives of the West. As for music, Balanchine was mainly faithful to Stravinsky, but also used compositions by such modern European composers as Auric, Milhaud, Ravel, and Sauguet. Prokofiev, a pupil of Tcherepnin (who had settled permanently in France) was the last representative of the more Russian element. The male and female dancers who were connected with the Diaghilev company over the years form too long a list to enumerate in full. A few of the outstanding performers were: Pierre Vladimiroff, Lydia Lopokova, Lubov Tchernicheva, Leon

Woizikovsky, Stanislas Idzikovsky, Vera Nemchinova, Alexandra Danilova, Alicia Markova (English), Anton Dolin (English), Serge Lifar, Anatole Vilzak, Olga Spessivtseva, and Vera Trefilova. Diaghilev also had available the services of the great teacher Cecchetti.

A main feature of all the Diaghilev ballets, which were spectacular dramatic works, was the emphasis, at least during the first period, upon pantomime and mimicry. The Russian school, especially in Moscow, always placed great stress on the portrayal of the narrative and dramatic elements. This emphasis was particularly beneficial to the narrative ballets in the Diaghilev repertory. Another source of strength lay in Diaghilev's greater interest in male than in female dancers; in his productions the latter were not so predominant as in the chief ballets of the West.

The Russian fables brought onto Western stages by Diaghilev were acclaimed by enthusiastic audiences. Several of these works remain in the repertory, but today, unfortunately, they are generally presented as wishy-washy extracts. Only companies with well-filled treasuries and splendidly trained soloists can venture revivals of his ballets. When all is said and done, what Diaghilev really brought to western Europe was Russian music, painting, and dancers, but very little dance art. And yet, even though the story about a new flowering of the ballet is but a myth, we have inherited from his works a great deal more substantial than this myth. Diaghilev died in Venice in 1929, whereupon his company broke up, and his dancers and assistants settled in Europe and the United States. Some of them set up companies of their own, such as Mordkin (whose troupe later became Ballet Theatre, now known as American Ballet Theatre) and Léonide Massine; others became advisors (Grigoriev) or ballet masters (N. Beriosov). A large number went into teaching, with the result that the present generation of dancers has been trained, and is still being trained, on the basis of Russian principles.

A final note on Diaghilev's behalf must be added. According to Ernest Ansermet, the conductor, it is an injustice to Diaghilev to say that his work was limited to colorful ballets. In his later years, Ansermet holds, Diaghilev already was oriented toward "abstract" ballet, and as proof he points to Diaghilev's hiring of Balanchine as choreographer. What this might have meant cannot be determined, for Diaghilev's passing at only fifty-seven years of age cut short any possibility of confirming Ansermet's assertion.

BALLETS

The Firebird ("L'Oiseau de Feu")

Ballet in three scenes. Book and choreography: Michel Fokine. Music: Igor Stravinsky. Scenery and costumes: Alexander Golovin. Costume of the Firebird and the princess: Léon Bakst. Première: June 25, 1910, at the Opéra, Paris, danced by the Serge Diaghilev Ballets Russes.

CHARACTERS: Firebird; Prince Ivan; the Tsarevna; the evil enchanter Kastchei; bewitched princesses; followers and prisoners of the enchanter; pages; young people.

SCENE 1.

After the overture, designed to create a fairy-tale mood, the curtain goes up, revealing a portion of Kastchei's forest and a tree full of golden apples. Suddenly a beautiful luminescent bird flies through the woods. Prince Ivan enters by climbing over an old wall, at the left. He shoots an arrow at the bird but misses. After watching the bird a while, he decides to capture it alive. With some difficulty he finally gets it in his arms. Firebird struggles to free herself, and finally offers one of her golden feathers as ransom. Ivan accepts, and lets Firebird go. She flies off, leaving Ivan alone.

SCENE 2.

Through a huge gate at the left of the stage come twelve princesses and the lovely Tsarevna, all captives of the evil sorcerer Kastchei. The girls playfully shake the tree with the golden apples, retrieve the apples that fall, and play a game of catch. The princesses do a very old folk dance formerly danced by girls in honor of the goddess of love. Prince Ivan watches from the side, enchanted. When he comes closer, the girls discover his presence and shriek. The Tsarevna warns him to go away, because he is in the enchanter's forest. But Prince Ivan has fallen in love with the Tsarevna and chooses to remain. Suddenly the sound of a trumpet is heard. The girls flee to the sorcerer's castle, and Prince Ivan is left alone. He tries to escape but finds the gate closed; despite all his efforts, he can not open it. He looks around, uncertainly. Monstrous figures, followers of the sorcerer, then open the gate, seize the prince, and hold him fast until Kastchei enters. Kastchei looks at his new captive curiously. Prince Ivan tries to free himself, but the odds against him are too great. Suddenly he remembers the golden feather, which he now takes out of his belt, and Firebird miraculously appears. She draws the followers of the sorcerer along in a wild dance at the end of which they all fall down exhausted and go to sleep. Then she shows the prince a tree stump in which the sorcerer's soul is hidden. Ivan pulls a large iron chest from the stump, opens it, and discovers a large egg inside. He throws the egg in the air, intending to catch it as it comes down, but the egg falls to the ground and breaks. Darkness envelops the stage.

Scene 3.

A number of nobles with their retinue pay homage to Prince Ivan. Pages offer him a crown, a scepter, and a fire-red cape to show that they recognize him as their ruler. The Tsarevna appears and is presented with a loaf of bread, which symbolizes the people's wish for a fruitful marriage between the prince and his beloved.

Michel Fokine assembled this story from various Russian fables. Diaghilev originally asked Anatole Liadov to write the music for the ballet, but when Liadov replied that the composition would require a year, Diaghilev withdrew the commission and gave it to Stravinsky, who worked in close collaboration with Fokine. At the première Karsavina danced the role of Firebird; Fokine, the prince; Enrico Cecchetti, the evil enchanter; and Vera Fokina, the Tsarevna. The original costumes and décors were lost, and Nathalie Gontcharova designed new ones in 1926.

On November 27, 1949, the New York City Center gave a new version of Stravinsky's composition, with choreography by George Balanchine. Maria Tallchief danced the Firebird and

Francisco Moncion, the prince. The sumptuous settings (costumes and curtain) had been designed by Marc Chagall for an earlier unsuccessful revival of the work by Adolph Bolm for Ballet Theatre in 1945. Whereas Fokine's production was splendidly staged and somewhat static, Balanchine's version is considerably more *dansant* and, thanks to Chagall's settings, has more of a fairy-tale atmosphere.

Serge Lifar staged *The Firebird* at the Paris Opéra in 1954, with Nina Vyroubova and Youly Algaroff in the leading roles.

The Sadler's Wells Ballet première performance of *The Firebird* dedicated to the memory of Diaghilev occurred on August 23, 1954. Margot Fonteyn and Michael Somes danced the principal roles.

Le Spectre de la Rose

Ballet in one act. Book: J. L. Vaudoyer, after a poem by Théophile Gautier. Choreography: Michel Fokine. Music: Carl Maria von Weber ("Invitation to the Waltz"). Scenery and costumes: Léon Bakst. Première: April 19, 1911, at the Théâtre de Monte Carlo, by the Serge Diaghilev Ballets Russes.

CHARACTERS: a young girl; the Spirit of the Rose.

The scene is a girl's bedroom. The woodwork is painted white and the wallpaper blue, with white flowers. Between long high windows, at the rear of the center stage, is a sofa covered in a pale blue material. To the right, in an alcove, is a bed, with covers turned back for the night. In the right foreground, next to a round table with a large vase, stands an empty armchair. To the left is a dressing table with sundry articles neatly arranged. Through the open windows one can see a garden full of flowering shrubs, bathed in moonlight. The moon also shines into the room, blending a greenish-yellow light on the floor.

A young girl returns from a ball. She is wearing a cape to protect her from the evening chill, and in her hand she carries a rose. She looks at the rose pensively, then brings it to her lips and kisses it. She takes off her cape, revealing a lovely cream-colored dance frock. She sits down in the armchair, closes her eyes dreamily, and falls asleep. The flower drops to the floor. Then, with a tremendous leap through the left window, the Spirit of the Rose, dressed in pink tights embroidered with green leaves, enters. He dances through the room with long light leaps. The girl joins him and together they dance a waltz. Finally she sinks back into the armchair. The Spirit of the Rose bends over her for a moment and then disappears with a great leap through the window by which he had entered.

The girl gradually awakens. Has she been dreaming, or was her experience real? She sees the fallen rose and picks it up carefully. A smile comes over her face. She presses the rose tenderly to her breast. The curtain falls.

This is a romantic ballet—because of the spirit, because of the apparition, because of the soaring leaps. Fokine did his best to contrast manly strength and womanly charm in this work, which was designed as a long *pas de deux* especially for Nijinsky (with Thamar Karsavina as the girl) so that the great dancer could display his phenomenal elevation to greatest advantage. Cyril Beaumont, who saw the première, says that a peak of excellence was reached that has never since been equaled—for setting, technique, or expression. The performance was a sensation, and the enthusiasm was so great at one benefit performance at the Paris Opéra that the entire ballet had to be repeated.

Fokine mounted this work afterwards for several dance groups, such as the Ballet Theatre. Nowadays many inferior performances of it are given and even amateur groups venture to present a version more or less of their own.

Petrouchka

Ballet in four scenes. Book: Igor Stravinsky and Alexandre Benois. Choreography: Michel Fokine. Music: Igor Stravinsky. Scenery and costumes: Alexandre Benois. Première: June 13, 1911, at the Théâtre du Châtelet, Paris, by the Serge Diaghilev Ballets Russes.

CHARACTERS: Petrouchka; the Ballerina; the Moor; the Charlatan; coachmen; nursemaids; two street dancers; two gypsy girls; a merchant; two drummers; a barrel-organ man; an old man; revelers; holiday crowd; children; policemen; man with a bear.

SCENE 1. The square in front of the Admiralty in St. Petersburg. A fine winter day just before Lent around 1830. Left, a tent with a high platform. Next to it, a table with a large samovar. Center rear, the charlatan's tent with its puppets. In the background, the outlines of a merry-go-round with wooden horses; and in the distance, the dome of a church.

A festival is taking place. Into the square come the merrymakers —citizens, peasants, and countryfolk—out on a spree before the forty-day Lenten fast begins. An old man appears on the platform above the tent and tries to draw attention to his long white beard. Several women are having their fortunes told by gypsy women. A number of peasants are dancing to the melody of an accordion. A street dancer enters and does a dance to the tunes of a barrel organ. Another dancer performs while accompanying herself on a triangle. Each tries to outdo the other. Tipsy revelers run across the square. The Charlatan thrusts his head out of his tent, and then he emerges with his flute. He pulls the curtain of his tent aside revealing his three puppets: from left to right, the Moor, the Ballerina, and Petrouchka. The Moor is a vain, pretentious figure with wide breeches and a great ostrich feather sticking out. The gay Ballerina seems to be more interested in pleasing herself than others. Petrouchka, his head hanging low, is the sorrowful Russian Pierrot. At a sign from the Charlatan the puppets begin to dance, first in the tent and then in the snow in front of the tent. The Ballerina flirts with the Moor. Petrouchka is jealous. At a sign from the Charlatan the movements of the puppets become more enchanted, like those of marionettes. Then darkness falls.

SCENE 2. Petrouchka's three-cornered cell, which has blue walls. To the left, a low door.

The door is suddenly thrown open, the Charlatan kicks Petrouchka into the cell and then closes the door behind him. Alone and in despair, Petrouchka helplessly beats on the walls, trying vainly to find an opening and escape his puppet world—his limitations.

Then the Ballerina comes in. She looks on with amusement at Petrouchka's pitiful efforts. Petrouchka tries to entice the Ballerina by making handsome leaps, but she shows no interest in him and leaves. Petrouchka again seeks a way out; finally disconsolate and exhausted, he sinks down on the floor. The light goes out.

SCENE 3. The Moor's luxurious room, furnished almost voluptuously, with red hangings, enormous palm trees, and fruits. A divan somewhat to the left of center. Right, a picture of a snake.

As the curtain rises, the Moor is lying on the divan, playing with a coconut which he tries to crack. He pretends the coconut is an idol and begins to worship it. At that moment the Ballerina, holding a toy trumpet, enters the room. The Moor, surprised, drops the coconut and pursues the Ballerina. His advances are about to be accepted when Petrouchka appears. The Moor drives him from the room, and then takes the Ballerina on his knee.

SCENE 4. The square.

Merrymakers cross the square. Nine nursemaids do a dance to the music of an accordion. A rich merchant passes by with a gypsy on each arm. Some coachmen dance, and then the nursemaids dance with the coachmen. Masked figures enter.

At the height of the gaiety cries are heard, and the flap of the Charlatan's tent is violently shaken. Petrouchka comes out, pursued by the Moor who has a sword in his hand. The Ballerina follows the two rivals. The Moor strikes Petrouchka down, and the crowd attacks the assailant. Then, police are summoned. The Charlatan appears and shows everyone that Petrouchka is only a sawdust puppet, and hence has no soul; the people are satisfied and leave. The Charlatan takes the puppet and drags it behind him. Suddenly a scream is heard from the roof of the tent. The Charlatan terrified looks up and sees the torso of Petrouchka, which gesticulates. The Charlatan drops what he was carrying and runs off in terror.

☙

Petrouchka was the result of close collaboration between Stravinsky and Benois. Fokine incorporated well-known folk dances into his choreography, and took great care with the staging. Benois' décor and costumes were colorful and heightened the theatrical effect. At the première the roles of Petrouchka, the Ballerina, the Moor, and the Charlatan were taken by Vaslav Nijinsky, Thamar Karsavina, Alexander Orlov, and Enrico Cecchetti, respectively. It is worth noting that after the Paris première a Frenchman appeared backstage and claimed composer's royalties on the tune that Stravinsky had used for his barrel-organ scene. It is generally assumed that Stravinsky had heard the melody in Russia, where barrel organs frequently played Western melodies. Balanchine, who relates this anecdote, has unfortunately forgotten the name of the Frenchman.

In 1925 Fokine staged *Petrouchka* for the Royal Danish Ballet at Copenhagen. He also staged the first performances for the Original Ballet Russe in 1940, and for the Ballet Theatre in 1942. After the death of Fokine in 1942, Léonide Massine and Nicholas Beriosov mounted the work for several companies. In 1957, the Royal Ballet in London gave a revival of *Petrouchka*. Alexander Grant danced Petrouchka and Margot Fonteyn the Ballerina. Benois designed the settings and costumes.

The Afternoon of a Faun* ("L'Après-midi d'un Faune")

Ballet in one act. Book and choreography: Vaslav Nijinsky. Music: Claude Debussy. Scenery and costumes: Léon Bakst. Première: May 29, 1912, at the Théâtre du Châtelet, Paris, by the Serge Diaghilev Ballets Russes.

CHARACTERS: a faun, seven nymphs.

❧

A faun, sitting on a hillock one warm summer day, is playing his flute. A group of nymphs pass by the foot of the hill on their way to bathe. The faun is curious and starts to follow them. The nymphs are curious too, and at the same time a little more fearful of the faun; they run away. One of them, however, overpowered by curiosity, returns. The faun and the nymph reach out to each

* See page 172 for contemporary version.

other; the nymph becomes frightened again and flees, leaving her veil behind. Torn between her desire to retrieve her veil and her fear of the faun, she hesitates a moment. Finally, she departs without the veil. The faun remains behind, disconsolate. He picks up the veil and comforts himself by caressing the thin gauze as if it were the nymph.

The book and the choreography have always been publicly attributed to Nijinsky, but Igor Stravinsky states that the book was by Diaghilev, in conjunction with Bakst. Nijinsky's wife denies this contention and credits her husband with the idea and the setting. According to her, Nijinsky was inspired by pictures on ancient Greek vases.

At the première, many in the audience were shocked by the last part, in which the faun made what they considered indecent movements with the veil. His movements were indeed too explicit; it would have been far better to leave something to the spectator's imagination. In later performances, the ending of the ballet was toned down.

Serge Lifar also mounted a version of *L'Après-midi d'un Faune* in which the nymphs are omitted.

La Boutique Fantasque

Ballet in one act. Book and choreography: Léonide Massine. Music: Gioacchino Rossini, arranged by Ottorino Respighi. Scenery and costumes: André Derain. Première: June 5, 1919, at the Alhambra Theatre, London, by the Serge Diaghilev Ballets Russes.

CHARACTERS: a shopkeeper; his assistant; two servants; a young thief; two English ladies; an American couple, accompanied by their son and daughter; a Russian merchant, his wife, four daughters, and their young son; two tarantella dancers; queen of clubs; queen of hearts; king of diamonds; king of spades; a snob and his gardener; five Cossacks and their officers; a Cossack girl; two poodles; two cancan dancers; twelve girls.

❦

After a brief overture, the curtain rises, disclosing a luxurious doll shop, brightly illuminated. At the side of the shop is a storeroom.

The shopkeeper and his assistant enter the shop. The assistant dusts the dolls and arranges their clothes. He goes into the side room, and at that moment a poorly dressed boy slips into the shop and reaches for a gold ribbon belonging to one of the dolls. The assistant discovers the rascal in time; there is a struggle, and the boy escapes. As he is running out the door, he crashes into two English ladies, who become frightened and open their umbrellas in defense. After the boy has disappeared and the ladies feel that the danger has passed, they enter the shop with dignity.

The shopkeeper greets them with deep bows. The ladies ask to see some dolls, and the shopkeeper sets some mechanical dolls in motion. The ladies are pleased, and they ask to see more dolls. Other potential buyers, this time an American family, appear. The American complacently asks for a demonstration so that he may decide whether the dolls are worth considering for his children. Meanwhile, the boy and girl roam around the shop and finger the dolls. Their parents scold them and tell them to sit on chairs and behave like well-mannered children. The shopkeeper has his assistant bring in the tarantella dancers, who perform to the music of a tambourine. The children become excited, take the ladies by the hand, and try to imitate the dance they have just seen. Exhausted, the ladies sink into chairs and the parents scold the children for misbehaving. Four dolls dressed as playing cards do a mazurka, while the American beats time with his pipe. The ladies move around on their chairs as if they, too, were mechanical dolls. The children swing their legs and clap their hands. A Russian merchant enters with his family, as a march is being played. Those present are clearly not pleased by the new arrival. The English ladies think that the time has come to go and try to take the American family along with them, but the Americans decide to remain. The two English ladies leave rather disdainfully. Meanwhile the busy servants bring more dolls into the shop. The snob and the man with the melons do a comedy dance to the tunes of a music box.

The American and Russian families make the best of a bad

bargain and finally get acquainted with each other, as the children become wilder and wilder. They discover a number of dolls under a green cloth and ask whether they may see them too. A Cossack officer, his men, and a charming Cossack girl march in and perform a dance. After the officer has found an opportunity to give the girl a kiss, this dance ends. Then the shopkeeper himself comes out with two poodles, a large male and a female, holding them by the ears so that they can walk along on their hind feet. The male, a self-satisfied animal, growls contentedly and dances around the female. The American and his wife turn away from this spectacle and try to blindfold their children fearing that they might discover that the passions of people coincide with the passions of animals!

The shopkeeper now declares that all he has left to show are his favorite cancan dancers. The children are enthusiastic about these dolls, for they love the high-kicking ballerina and the leaping male dancer. Happily, there is no dispute as to who shall have which doll because the American children prefer the male dancer and the Russian children the ballerina. The two fathers ask the price of the dolls, and the shopkeeper, who does not like to turn over his favorite dolls to others, sets a high price. The fathers agree to pay the sum requested and arrange to call for the dolls the next morning. The cancan dancers are wrapped up and placed near the door. After the customers leave, the owner and his assistant dance a joyful waltz and close the shop. Darkness falls.

Now is the time when the dolls come to life. All enter and dance with each other until daybreak. The next morning when the shop opens, the two families appear in order to pick up their purchases. The shopkeeper and his assistant reach for the boxes, but find them empty! The new owners are outraged, the American hits the shopkeeper with his cane, while the poor assistant tries to hold the children off. Both families rush into the back room to break everything in sight, but the dolls put up resistance. The Russian's wife hurries back, pursued by the barking poodles; the merchant and his daughters are threatened by the playing cards. The American abandons the field to the cancan dancer, who kicks her legs scandalously high into the air. With the help of the Cossacks, both families are finally driven from the shop. Outside, the families look through the window at the delighted dolls doing a dance of joy with the owner inside the shop. The cancan dancer kicks her leg high in the air once more as the curtain falls.

❧

La Boutique Fantasque can be ranked among the first of Massine's youthful productions. He borrowed the subject from an old German ballet, and he made a study of the drawings of Toulouse-Lautrec for the setting. The subject shows some similarity to that of *Coppélia* because of the theme of the mechanical dolls.

At the première in 1919, the principal roles of the cancan dancers were taken by Lydia Lopokova and Léonide Massine; Enrico Cecchetti was the shopkeeper and Serge Grigoriev, the Russian merchant. The work has since been greeted with enthusiasm in many countries and has been taken into the repertories of various companies. Massine also mounted a version for the Sadler's Wells Ballet, which first presented the work at Covent Garden in 1947, with Massine and Moira Shearer as the cancan dancers.

In the United States, the Ballet Russe de Monte Carlo premiére took place on March 20, 1935, with Alexandra Danilova and Massine appearing as the cancan dancers.

The Three-Cornered Hat ("La Tricorne")

Ballet in one act. Book: Martinez Sierra after a fable by Alarcón. Choreography: Léonide Massine. Music: Manuel de Falla. Scenery, curtain, and costumes: Pablo Picasso. Première: July 22, 1919, at the Alhambra Theatre, London, by the Serge Diaghilev Ballets Russes.

CHARACTERS: the miller; his wife; the corregidor (magistrate); his wife; the dandy; peasants; village idiots; men and women; police; beggars; the voice of a singer.

❧

The curtain parts revealing a drop curtain which depicts a bull-fight and spectators. The orchestra plays a sort of *entrada*, with clapping, stamping of feet, the playing of castanets, cries of *olé*, and the voice of a singer.

The second curtain rises, disclosing on the left, the miller's house; in the center rear, a bridge with high arches; and on the right, a mill worked by a water wheel. On the wall of the mill hang a bird cage and a shotgun. To the left of the house are a well and a bucket. The sky is a brilliant deep blue.

The miller, in tight-fitting breeches and a blouse, stands in front of his house, playing with a bird. He shows the bird that the sundial points to two o'clock and whistles twice to the bird; the bird in turn whistles three times. At this moment the miller's wife comes out, coquettishly smoothing her dress. She sees her husband and makes fun of his efforts to teach the bird; she will show him that she can do better. She feeds the bird, and it whistles twice. The miller's wife is pleased and dances a *koradin* with her husband. But the miller has more to do than dance; he must water the flowers. He draws a bucket of water from the well and gives the bird some water. Meanwhile, his wife notices a finely-clad dandy on the bridge, playing with a kite on a string. The dandy looks with pleasure on the miller's pretty wife and does a few bolero steps to attract her attention. She returns his greeting, but her husband observes this flirtatious play and runs down angrily to the bridge; the dandy leaves. The miller's wife, glad her husband is jealous, laughingly assures him that she cares for him alone.

The music indicates that something special is about to take place. This turns out to be the arrival of the corregidor's wife, who is carried in a sedan chair and accompanied by the old corregidor on foot. When the procession reaches the miller's house, it halts for a moment; the corregidor drops his handkerchief, and the miller's wife picks it up and returns it to him with a coquettish bow. The corregidor's wife does not find her husband's attitude toward the miller's wife everything that it should be and orders the porters to move on.

The miller and his wife are left alone, and now it is the miller's turn to make his wife a little jealous. Four men bring in heavy sacks of grain; a pretty young woman enters with a jug on her shoulder. The miller blows kisses to the young woman with abandon. The wife makes a scene and bursts into tears. The miller says that he loves only her. Their reconciliation is sealed with embraces and kisses.

Music in the distance announces the return of the corregidor. The miller, a little angry because he thinks that the corregidor wants to court his wife, enters the house, but the miller's wife stays behind to await the corregidor and his procession. She begins to dance a fandango by herself. So absorbed is she in her dancing that she does not notice the presence of the corregidor, who admires the pretty steps and turns without concealing his desire. The miller's wife suddenly notices the corregidor watching and beating time on the ground with his ebony cane. She tells him that she is greatly honored to have him watch her. Her friendliness makes the corregidor forget himself, and he pats her under the chin. With a few minuet steps, he invites her to dance. She dances for a moment, but prefers the freer folk dance to the formal steps. Continuing her flirtation, she takes a bunch of grapes and teasingly holds it out to the corregidor; a chase ensues. The miller's wife takes the grapes in her snow-white teeth and dances provocatively before the corregidor. The old man reaches for her, but she is too quick, and he never succeeds in getting hold of her or the grapes. Finally, in a desperate last attempt, he lunges, loses his balance, and falls to the ground exhausted. The miller, who has watched the entire proceedings from the house, comes out and, with his wife's help, lifts the old man up. For him, the grapes have turned out to be rather sour.

Uttering maledictions, the corregidor leaves. The miller and his wife, having found each other again, are unconcerned about the old man's revenge; they dance a fandango. But the corregidor is determined to have the miller's pretty wife. If one is not strong, one must be crafty!

Peasants and villagers arrive to celebrate a noonday fiesta in honor of the solstice. The miller's wife greets everyone, and after the new arrivals have danced briefly, the miller begins his *farruca* (the well-known Miller's Dance, often executed by Spanish soloists). Everyone greets the miller with loud applause when he finishes. A barrel of wine is brought. Glasses are filled and emptied.

Some gendarmes appear, apparently to spoil the feast. Their leader takes out a large scroll, and one of the gendarmes lights a lantern because it is already getting dark. The paper is unrolled and read aloud; it is an order for the arrest of the miller. At a loss to know what he has done, the miller asks for an explanation, but the gendarmes can not give it to him. They were merely ordered to arrest him, and summarily they take him away. The joy is over, the merrymakers leave, and the miller's wife is left alone.

The cuckoo clock strikes eight; the bird in the cage chirps nine times. The wife retires to her bedroom, but does not stay there long, for she can not sleep. She goes outside, glances around, and walks to the bridge, looking left and right. She sees nothing, and then sits weeping on the bridge. The corregidor, however, has had the miller arrested so that he himself could have the miller's wife for himself, and he returns surreptitiously. He throws off his great cape in order to reach her more quickly, hurries up the bridge, and embraces her. She shrieks, defends herself stoutly, and shoves the corregidor, who falls into the water. He climbs up the bank dripping wet, but the cold bath does not seem to have cooled his ardor. He goes after the miller's pretty wife once more. In her desperation, the wife snatches a shotgun and drives the obnoxious old man off; then she quickly leaves.

The corregidor begins to realize the futility of the situation and his own discomfort. He takes off his wet clothes and goes into the miller's house to look for dry clothing.

The miller, however, has succeeded in escaping from jail and has returned home. He sees the corregidor's cape, picks it up, and throws it over the bird cage. Then he draws a caricature of the corregidor on the wall of his house. (In some versions he inscribes the motto, "Your wife is not less beautiful than mine.") Gathering up the corregidor's wet clothes, which he takes with him, he leaves the house to look for his wife. Meanwhile the corregidor has put on the miller's clothes, and has begun to feel more comfortable. His well-being is short-lived, however, for the gendarmes have discovered the miller's escape and, returning to look for him, mistake the corregidor for the escaped prisoner. They seize the corregidor and treat him rather roughly. At this moment the miller's wife returns with the villagers. She sees the corregidor and, thinking him to be her husband, starts to intercede; then the miller enters with a troupe of merrymakers. They have made a straw man dressed in the corregidor's wet clothes, and they throw it back and forth. The holiday rejoicing, so cruelly broken a few hours earlier, is restored. The miller is free; the corregidor has been overthrown. All dance a jota, mocking the straw figure of the corregidor on the bridge.

❦

Although he already had an extensive repertory, Diaghilev, who had long wanted to do something Spanish, took advantage of a tour to Spain during the First World War to begin work on a Spanish ballet. Massine, Diaghilev, and De Falla (who had been commissioned to prepare the score) went to seldom-frequented spots in Andalusia for inspiration. They watched native dancers in cafés and listened to folk music. An example of the results of this research is De Falla's incorporation in the score of a melody taken from a blind guitar player, whose name is unknown.

The subject matter of *The Three-Cornered Hat* is not so well suited for a ballet as, for example, that of *Le Beau Danube*. On the other hand, Massine did succeed in finding an acceptable form into which to fit the flirtatious wife, her beloved husband, and the old corregidor who is made to appear a trifle too silly. Every dance movement is meaningful, and the action and the dances are logically fused together.

Picasso's magnificent setting, which employs mainly light colors, sets off the dance figures nicely. The costumes, however, are occasionally too comical and more fussy than need be.

The music and story had already been performed as a pantomime in Madrid in 1917, under the title *El Corregidor y la Molinera*, a *farsa mimica*. But De Falla changed the score considerably for the ballet, and added the jota at the end.

At the première in 1919, Massine himself danced the principal role, Thamar Karsavina was the miller's wife, and Leon Woizikovsky was the corregidor. The work is currently in the repertory of several ensembles. In 1958 at the Holland Festival, the sixty-two-year-old Massine once more danced the principal role in the ballet, while his fifteen-year-old daughter Tatiana danced the role of the wife.

The Prodigal Son ("Le Fils Prodigue")

Ballet in three scenes. Book: Boris Kochno. Choreography: George Balanchine. Music: Serge Prokofiev. Scenery and costumes: Georges

Rouault. Première: May 20, 1929, at the Théâtre Sarah Bernhardt, Paris, by the Serge Diaghilev Ballets Russes.

CHARACTERS: the prodigal son; the father; two sisters; two friends; the siren; comrades.

SCENE 1. Outside the front door of the father's house. Right, the father's dwelling; left, a tent belonging to the son.

Friends are busy gathering roots and fruits in preparation for the trip they are to make with the son. The son, followed by his sisters, comes out of the tent that he has put up to accustom himself to a traveler's dwelling. The girls try to convince him of something, but he pays no attention. He dances to express his joy over the coming trip, but stops when his father comes out of the house. The father is sorry that the son wants to leave and tries to convince him of the dependability and happiness of a fixed abode. The son rejects this advice and perseveres in his decision to go. He wants desperately to leave his confining house and to go into the world. The preparations for his trip are over; the son and friends depart as the father looks after them sorrowfully.

SCENE 2. A country far away. A banquet hall with a great table and many chairs. Left, the tent.

A rather wild-looking group of men enter to march music. They sit down at the table, drink, and then dance. The son and his two friends arrive at the barbarous feast. In a little while the siren enters and dances seductively to Oriental music; the men look on, aroused with desire.

At the high point of the dance the son jumps up to join her. Now the siren performs for the prodigal alone. A dance by the two friends follows, and then there is a *pas de deux* by the siren and the son. The drunken merrymakers attack the siren and the son. The table is overturned and the chairs knocked about. They overpower the son, take his clothes, and leave. The son, left alone, sees their deceit and his own self-deception and performs a dance indicating repentance. Then the so-called friends return with the siren. The canvas of the tent is fastened to the overturned table for a sail. With the siren serving as its figurehead the ship conjured up in this way sails off with the false friends.

SCENE 3. Outside the father's house.

The son stretches his hand out longingly. His two sisters, who come by, at first mistake him for a beggar. The father comes out of the house and sees the returned son, who kneels repentantly before him. Deeply ashamed, the son starts to leave. The father takes the son into his arms, forgives him, and carries him into the house.

~

The story, generally believed to have been taken from Luke 15:11-24, was more probably inspired by Byzantine icons. The dramatic ballet is rather unsatisfying when compared with the biblical text. The jealous brother, surely a main character, is omitted in the ballet, and in his place two sisters are introduced. The emphasis is on the banquet scene in the far country. Although the costumes are often attributed to Rouault (who actually designed the scenery), they should be credited more properly to Diaghilev and Vera Arturovna Stravinsky, who, using Rouault's sketches, put them together hurriedly just before the première. The roles of the prodigal son, the siren, and the father were danced by Serge Lifar, Felia Dubrovska, and Michael Fedorov, respectively.

In 1939 David Lichine created his own version of Balanchine's ballet for the Original Ballet Russe. Lichine played the role of the prodigal son; Sono Osato was the siren.

George Balanchine added his work to the repertory of the New York City Center, with Jerome Robbins and Maria Tallchief as the principals. In recent years the role of the prodigal son has been danced with particular distinction by Edward Villella.

Du Feu de son Génie il anima la Danse:
Au beau jours de la Grèce il sut la rapeller.
Et recouvrant par lui leur antique Eloquence
Les Gestes et les Pas aprirent à parler.

1. JEAN GEORGES NOVERRE

2. MARIUS PETIPA

Photo: Fred Fehl

3. THE BLACK SWAN
(Alicia Alonso and Igor Youskevitch)

Sadler's Wells Theatre Ballet

Photo: Angus McBean

4. *THE NUTCRACKER*

Marquis de Cuevas Ballet

Photo : Serge Lido

5. *THE PRISONER OF THE CAUCASUS*

6. *MISS JULIE*
(Kirsten Simone and Erik Bruhn)

7. *THE FIREBIRD*

(Maria Tallchief and Francisco Moncion)

8. *FANCY FREE*

9. RODEO

10. *THE AFTERNOON OF A FAUN*
(Patricia McBride and Francisco Moncion)

11. *AGON*

12. GEORGE BALANCHINE
(with Melissa Hayden and Roland Vazquez
in a rehearsal of *A Midsummer Night's Dream*)

6

The Contemporary Ballet

With Diaghilev's passing in 1929 an era came to an end; indeed many regarded Diaghilev's death as a disaster from which ballet would probably never recover. Shortly thereafter Anna Pavlova also passed from the scene, and her dance art was lost to the world. But it was to the credit of both these leading figures that ballet, so greatly revived and stimulated in Europe and America as a result of their efforts, would not fade into oblivion. Artists from both the Diaghilev and the Pavlova dance groups, mainly Russians who had joined these groups after leaving their homeland following the Revolution, remained to carry on, and since then they have made significant contributions to the development of ballet art throughout the Western world.

FRANCE

In France, where the Paris Opéra had tried to maintain the old traditions of ballet, somnolence had set in by the end of the nineteenth century. Neither Louis Mérante (*maître de ballet* and choreographer from 1848 to 1887) nor Leo Staats (*maître de ballet* and choreographer from 1909 to 1936) were able to inspire popular interest.

105

After Diaghilev, the leading figure in Paris was the Russian ex-patriate Serge Lifar. Appointed ballet master and choreographer in 1932, he failed to win acceptance by most of the French nationalists. Lifar has always been a controversial figure in the ballet world, although, from an international point of view, he has never been an innovator. He must have been so regarded in Paris, however, where his brief insistence that the ballet must be no longer dependent on music met with distinct disfavor. His ballet *Icare* (1935) was his first attempt to create a work on the basis of this conception, and for it he devised rhythms to conform to the movements of the dancers. It soon became apparent that ballet is unthinkable without music, or at least without the metrical divisions that music provides for dancers, and in due time Lifar abandoned this ill-advised approach. In addition to *Icare* Lifar composed a number of unimportant works, including *Alexandre le Grand* (1937) and *Nautéos* (1954), both of which had some success in their time. *Suite en blanc* (1943), a music ballet danced without settings is actually his only work that can still be put in repertory. Lifar's influence came to an end in 1958 when he retired from his position at the Opéra. Since then the Paris Opéra has shown signs of reviving—under the influence of Skibine, Balanchine, and Harald Lander.

After the Second World War, another group, the Ballets des Champs-Elysées, in revolt against the limitations of the Paris Opéra, came into prominence, stimulated by Boris Kochno (former adviser to Diaghilev), Irène Lidova, and the young impresario Claude Giraud. Roland Petit (1924–   ) and Janine Charrat (1924–   ) were the stars of the group. The dancers were attractive because of their youth and vigor, and some of them—for example Jean Babilée and Renée Jeanmaire—achieved world-wide renown. Important works during this period were: *Les Forains* (1945), *Le Jeune Homme et la Mort* (1946), *Les Demoiselles de la Nuit* (1948), and *Carmen* (1949)—all by Petit. Janine Charrat created *Jeu de Cartes* (1945), *Adam Miroir* (1948), *Abraxas* (1949), and a number of smaller ballets. These choreographers did not produce much that was new to the art of dance, but their works were well received—no doubt in large measure because of the contributions of the competent artists and the popular, modern composers.

In 1948 Roland Petit split off from the group, taking with him most of the dancers, in order to form his own company; whereupon, in 1950, the Ballets des Champs-Elysées ceased operations. Janine Charrat also formed a small company with which she has toured Europe and the rest of the world. Despite the recent work of several experimental groups, there have been no really important creations in French ballet, possibly because it is still too closely tied to eroticism.

DENMARK

In Denmark the Bournonville tradition still continued. Harald Lander (1905–   ) directed the Royal Danish Ballet in Copenhagen from 1932 to 1951. He developed many of today's dancers, upheld the old repertory, and contributed several ballets of his own, among them the fine *Études*. Guest choreographers from other countries complete the Danish repertory. The style of the dancers is marked by great suppleness, lightness, and beauty of line. There is no attempt made in Copenhagen to stun the audience by technique. Vera Volkova, who was trained in Russia by Vaganova and others, assumed responsibility for the training of dancers after Lander resigned. She is a splendid *maîtresse de ballet,* one with whom soloists are eager to work.

ENGLAND

Prior to the twentieth century, ballet in England was slow in developing as an art because, although there was a public interested in attending ballet performances, few actually wanted to study it and to perform! Recently, the progress of ballet in England has been stimulated by the artistry and support of Marie Rambert, Ninette de Valois, Adeline Genée (a longtime favorite of British audiences, who danced her farewell performance in 1914), and Thamar Karsavina (the great ballerina of Diaghilev's company).

Here we shall mention the special contributions of two of these gifted artists: Marie Rambert and Ninette de Valois. Marie Rambert (1888–   ) left Warsaw for Paris in order to study medicine, but soon changed her mind and went to Geneva where she trained with Jacques Dalcroze in music and eurythmics. She worked with Diaghilev after meeting him in Dresden, and then became a student of Enrico Cecchetti. Later she founded her own school and ballet company (Ballet Rambert); during the past forty years, she has earned a high reputation as a teacher and has encouraged and developed outstanding dancers and choreographers. Ninette de Valois (1898–   ), who danced with Diaghilev's company for two years, made her ensembles—namely, the Sadler's Wells Ballet and the Sadler's Wells Theatre Ballet—the foremost groups in England. In 1957 her work was rewarded by the granting of the name Royal Ballet to both groups. She has also choreographed a number of ballets, among the best of which are *Checkmate* (1937) and *Job* (1951).

Frederick Ashton is a choreographer of importance to British ballet. Born in Ecuador in 1906, Ashton was trained by Léonide Massine and Marie Rambert. The latter gave him an opportunity to work as a choreographer as early as 1926, and he was for a long time the only choreographer in England working with abstract ballet. Among the many ballets that Ashton created are: *Les Patineurs* (1937); *Dante Sonata* (1940); *Symphonic Variations* (1946); and *Homage to the Queen* (the Coronation Ballet of 1953). He also created some highly acclaimed full-length ballets: *Cinderella* (1948), *Tiresias* (1951), and *Sylvia* (1952), among others.

It is not yet possible to speak of a characteristic British style in choreography, but we can discern a certain use of long lines in space, perhaps a heritage of the Danish Bournonville school. The staging is good, but in general both the British choreographer and spectator seem to have great difficulty with abstract music ballets. The dramatic ballet, on the other hand, still reigns supreme. This is understandable in a country still immured in the Shakespearean tradition, but it is an inhibiting factor in the further development of the art of ballet.

GERMANY AND OTHER
CENTRAL EUROPEAN COUNTRIES

Germany has never made any great contribution to the ballet. Nonetheless, Germans were for a short time leaders in the dance art of western Europe. Their influence was particularly strong in the Netherlands, which had no ballet tradition, and later in England as well, especially in the sphere of modern dance. Rudolf von Laban (1879–1958), a native Hungarian, founded the Central European dance school, in which ballet technique was completely rejected and free body movements were advocated. Mary Wigman (1886–   ) and Kurt Jooss (1901–   ) were his most important disciples. Mary Wigman's tremendous stage personality gripped her audiences for many years; afterwards she became a teacher. She was the outstanding figure of German expressionism in the art of the dance, a movement that was (in Germany and Holland during the twenties and thirties) and is (in the United States today—e.g., Martha Graham) almost entirely practiced by women. These are dancers who "express themselves," believing that they can translate their deepest feelings directly into "dance." Wigman tried to give expression in her choreography to the "rising masses"—an attempt that failed completely.

Kurt Jooss was primarily a theater artist who addressed the world with an ideological message. *The Green Table* (set to music by Frederic Cohen and costumed by Hein Heckroth) will always remain the masterpiece of the dance of those years. This dance drama had its première in Paris on July 3, 1932, in a competition at the International Congress of the Dance, and won the first prize, deservedly. By 1947 it had already had over 3,200 performances. *The Green Table* had an unmistakable influence in the world of dance, particularly on British ballet, although it does not belong to the realm of ballet on *pointes*. In later years Kurt Jooss came to the conviction that no school and no dance system can be built on the basis of Laban's ideas, nor on any other fixed system, for that matter.

Like Germany, countries such as Belgium, Italy, Sweden, and others in Central Europe have a number of ballet groups and companies. But none of these countries has yet contributed significantly to the development of the art of ballet. Contemporary experiments in Germany and elsewhere are still on a somewhat expressionistic level.

RUSSIA

In Russia there was another flowering, after Petipa, under the Bolshoi ballet master Alexander Gorsky (1871–1924). An opponent of Petipa's conceptions, he laid great stress on pantomime in ballet. Agrippina Vaganova (1879–1951), who began teaching in 1919 and who was also artistic director of the Kirov Ballet (formerly the Maryinsky Ballet) from 1930–37, was probably the finest teacher during this century. Her ballet manual *Fundamentals of the Classic Dance* (published in Russia in 1943) is consulted by many dancers throughout the world.

A certain renaissance might have been expected in the Soviet Union after the Revolution. Actually, the main change was in subject matter; for a while everything had to have a socialist purpose and content. (Vaganova was the exception during this period; while director of the Kirov Ballet she never bothered to revise the old repertory and kept presenting it as it had always been performed.) But this extreme point of view was abandoned, and the old "classic"—that is, romantic—works were ultimately revived. In recent years, great attention has been given to training in expressive mime and dance movements; the Russian companies are, therefore, in a position to bring dramatic works to the stage as entire compositions. Choreographers and ballet masters who have contributed to Russian ballet are: Leonid Lavrovsky; Asaf Messerer; Igor Moiseyev; Mikhail Gabovich; Alexei Yermolayeff; Vasily Wainonen; Rostislav Zakharov; and Vakhtang Chaboukiani.

The technique of the contemporary Bolshoi dancers is amazing. The Bolshoi repertory is comprised almost exclusively of dramatic works in which the staging and the stage action play a great part. The structure of the work follows the subject of the action. There is an occasional solo, *pas de deux* or *pas de trois*, alternating with reconstructed folk dances executed by the *corps de ballet*. The Russians have not yet discovered pure, autonomous dance art.

THE UNITED STATES

The United States, where many Russian *émigrés* settled, has gone further than any other country in the development of pure dance, to which the Russian *émigrés* made outstanding contributions. After the First World War Fokine took up residence in New York and appeared there in 1922 with a number of his pupils. In 1924 he formed his own company, with which he appeared at the Metropolitan Opera House. In 1924–25, Anna Pavlova made her last American tour and in 1925 Mikhail Mordkin performed with a group called the Russian Ballet Company. The first performance of the Ballets Russes de Monte Carlo took place in 1933.

The School of American Ballet was opened in 1934, under the direction of George Balanchine. Later in the same year Balanchine presented a company of his own, sponsored by Lincoln Kirstein (who, although he always remained in the background, not being personally ambitious, as Diaghilev was, contributed a great deal to ballet, probably more than Diaghilev). By 1937 Mordkin had a fine company, which was taken over by Lucia Chase in 1940 and baptized Ballet Theatre, later American Ballet Theatre. In 1938 Massine assumed leadership of the Ballet Russe de Monte Carlo, which Sergei Denham took over in 1942. In 1940 Colonel de Basil's Original Ballet Russe performed in New York and has since made intermittent appearances in the United States. In 1945 Massine organized yet another company which performed under the name Ballet Russe Highlights. Not only were these companies formed by outstanding Russians, but most of the performers were also from Russia—although they were very soon supplemented by dancers trained in America.

During the thirties and forties, most of the companies presented both the old romantic repertory and the Diaghilev ballets. Finally, out of these many ensembles, two groups crystallized which developed their own specific tendencies: the American Ballet Theatre and the New York City Ballet.

The American Ballet Theatre, under the leadership of Lucia Chase and Oliver Smith, has developed a typically "American" character. Over the years it has built up its repertory to include dramatic ballets on American subjects, danced to music by American composers. Ballet Theatre has made an important contribution to the development of an American national ballet and has mirrored American life in the art of ballet in a highly dramatic manner. The works of Agnes de Mille and Jerome Robbins have had special significance in this development. After numerous financial difficulties, American Ballet Theatre, in 1962, moved from its former home in New York to Washington, D. C. where, as a resident company, its prospects seem much improved.

The New York City Ballet, which evolved from the School of American Ballet and Ballet Society and in 1948 received its present name and permanent home at the New York City Center, took a different road under its director George Balanchine. Balanchine became the champion of the art of abstract ballet, which had its roots in the music and painting of the early 1900's. In contrast to Lifar, Balanchine believes that ballet *cannot exist without music*. The choreographer and the dancers must always have a guide for the metrical and even the rhythmic-melodic division of time in order to be able to master space. A choreographer who rejects dramatic action can not derive his choreography from the course of the story (indeed, it is questionable whether this is ever possible) but must guide himself principally by the structure of the musical composition. In maintaining these principles, the choreographer understandably often chooses late Baroque music on the one hand or that of the later Stravinsky on the other.

From the outset of his career at the City Center, Balanchine objected to performing classical repertory. It took more than ten years to win a large segment of the public over to his conception, and there are still some dissenters. It was only after he had obtained a certain following that Balanchine offered his own setting of *Swan Lake* (1952), after Petipa, and a little later *The Nutcracker* (1954). In 1961 Balanchine added an elaborate full-length story ballet, *Midsummer Night's Dream*, to the repertory.

After first using the expression "abstract ballets," Balanchine changed it to "music ballets," which may well be more correct, for his works are always based entirely on the structure of the music. The form of his ballets is logically and geometrically constructed, a fact realized by every spectator. Balanchine rejects stage settings. In a Balanchine ballet we are able, undisturbed by settings and elaborate costumes, to enjoy the "measured construction in space, demonstrated by moving bodies set to certain patterns or sequence in rhythm and melody" (as Balanchine himself described his work *Agon* in December, 1957).

In Balanchine works the ballerina often remains the queen, but we get the impression that this is more a personal disposition than an artistic principle. *Four Temperaments* (1946), one of Balanchine's greatest masterworks, indicates that the function of the man and the woman are of equal value (an idea further developed by Balanchine in *Agon*).

Balanchine's ballets are the strongest expression of the "art of the ballet" and of what "art" means at all times and in all places. In this pure art we find ourselves in rarefied space, in the same realm of art as Bach and the late Stravinsky. As Balanchine says succinctly: "A lean style is our style."

Among the extensive repertory of George Balanchine ballets are: *Apollon Musagète*, Stravinsky (1928, 1943, 1951*); *The Prodigal Son*, Prokofiev (1929 and 1950); *Serenade*, Tchaikovsky (1934, 1935, and 1948); *Orpheus*, Gluck (1936) and Stravinsky (1948); *Concerto Barocco*, Bach (1941 and 1945); *Night Shadow*, Vittorio Rieti (1946); *Four Temperaments*, Paul Hindemith (1946); *Symphony in C*, Georges Bizet (1947 and

* Since Balanchine often makes considerable changes when mounting a work, the additional dates indicate new versions.

1948); *Firebird,* Stravinsky (1949); *Bourrée Fantasque,* Emmanuel Chabrier (1949); *Caracole,* Mozart (1952); *Western Symphony,* Hershy Kay (1954); *Agon,* Stravinsky (1957); and a handsome dramatic ballet (for Balanchine is also an excellent stage director): *Tyl Eulenspiegel,* Richard Strauss (1951).

Balanchine's pupils have included some of his young choreographers such as John Taras and Jerome Robbins. John Taras (1919–   ) attempted music ballets along Balanchine's principles with *Graziana* (1945), *Designs with Strings* (1948), *Tarasiana* (1951). Jerome Robbins (1918–   ) worked many years with Balanchine. His works, however, are not music ballets; they usually have a subject, a content, a mood, a tendency, or a comical or ludicrous idea. He does not operate with the excessive precision of Balanchine; his structure is less elaborate and mathematical, and more loosely free, American, and thus more refreshing. A difference in approach between these two choreographers is noteworthy, although minor in nature: at the end of almost every ballet Balanchine brings all his dancers on the stage and has the curtain fall before the entire company, whereas Robbins usually has everyone off stage before the curtain falls.

In addition to a number of musicals, Robbins has choreographed many ballets, including *Fancy Free,* Leonard Bernstein (1944); *Interplay,* Morton Gould (1945); *The Age of Anxiety,* Bernstein (1950); *Pied Piper,* Aaron Copland (1951); *The Cage,* Stravinsky (1951); *The Afternoon of a Faun,* Claude Debussy (1953); *The Concert,* Frederic Chopin (1958); and *N. Y. Export: Opus Jazz,* Robert Prince (1958).

Opinions vary with regard to the contributions made by various choreographers in the United States. Some Americans rate Martha Graham highly, while others shrug their shoulders. Undoubtedly she looked for new forms and found some, but nonetheless the great impression that she makes on certain people is almost entirely based on elements unrelated to the art of dance; her actual contribution, though small, lies in the expansion of the possibilities of expressive movement.

The position of Antony Tudor is somewhat special. He was trained by Marie Rambert, under whose direction he began to create ballets in England. He settled in America in 1939 and joined Ballet Theatre. As a choreographer Tudor always tries to express serious dramatic action in dance. His ballets, his atmosphere, and his drama have remained typically British; he has a tendency to feature adulterers or people who would like to be adulterous. His *Jardin aux Lilas* (1936), later called *Lilac Garden,* is his best attempt to express human drama in ballet movements. Much less successful is *Pillar of Fire,* which ranks in America as one of the most important ballet works. Here his stumbling block is the awkward improbability that any woman in a highly emotional state would suddenly start turning about on one toe.

Other choreographers who have made recent contributions are: Catherine Littlefield (1908–1951), who created a number of ballets between 1939 and 1940 and later choreographed musicals and ice revues; Ruth Page, who received her training from disciples of Diaghilev and has a group of her own from which she has created a number of dramatic ballets, including *Franky and Johnny* (1939), *Impromptu au Bois* (1952), and *La Revanche* (1952); Lew Christensen (1908–   ), who has created, among others, *Filling Station* (1938), *Jinx* (1942), and *Con Amore* (1953, in the repertory of the San Francisco Ballet); Eugene Loring, who choreographed *Billy the Kid* (1938); and Agnes de Mille, who first started working with Marie Rambert, later created a sensation with her choreography for the musical *Oklahoma!* (1943), and made important contributions to ballet, such as *Black Ritual* (Darius Milhaud, 1940), *Rodeo* (Aaron Copland, 1942), *Tally-Ho* (Gluck, 1944), and *Fall River Legend* (Morton Gould, 1948).

BALLETS

Les Présages

Choreographic symphony in four parts. Choreography: Léonide Massine. Music: Tchaikovsky's Fifth Symphony. Scenery and costumes: André Masson. Première: April 13, 1933, at Monte Carlo, by Colonel de Basil's Ballet Russe.

❧

The entire work is performed before a single backdrop painted in shades of red, yellow, brown, and green. On the right of the cloth is a frightening mask in profile, above which is a small cloud from which long-tailed meteors shoot forth.

PART I: Andante, allegro. Action, or life with its diversions, ambitions, and temptations.

A female soloist dances against a moving background of the *corps de ballet*. A *pas de trois* by one male dancer and two female dancers is sometimes inserted.

PART II: Andante cantabile. Passion, or the struggle between sacred and profane love.

A female soloist dances in turn with two contesting male dancers; one of these male dancers is "Fate." The contest also takes place against the background of the *corps de ballet*.

PART III: Allegro moderato. Frivolity.

A female soloist dances a waltz, followed by a group dance with an all-female *corps de ballet*.

PART IV: Andante maestoso, allegro vivace. War.

The destruction caused by war is expressed by all the soloists and in a group dance by the entire *corps de ballet*. In the end, good triumphs.

❧

In attempting to create a symphonic ballet, Massine over-reached his powers and was forced to seek a "handhold" in the struggle between good and evil. *Les Présages* is not a very strong ballet. Basically it shows little imagination, and Massine's treatment of space leaves much to be desired. Falling between two schools, the work today gives the impression of being very old-fashioned.

It is interesting that Massine himself stated (in the summer of 1958) that his ideal was to stage abstract ballets, but, he sighed, "they always ask for my older works."

Le Beau Danube

Ballet in one act. Book: Léonide Massine. Choreography: Léonide Massine. Music: Johann Strauss, orchestrated by Roger Desormière.

Backdrop: Vladimir Polunin, inspired by drawings of Constantin Guys. Costumes: Count Etienne de Beaumont. Première: April 15, 1933, at Monte Carlo, by the Ballets Russes de Monte Carlo.

CHARACTERS: street dancer; father; mother; daughter; hussar; barker; strong man; performers; first hand; dandy; painter; gardener; shop girls; dressmakers; ladies; gentlemen; young people.

The scene takes place on a Sunday in the Vienna Prater, about 1860.

As the splendid waltz music of Johann Strauss is heard, the curtain opens on a number of Sunday strollers. A gardener takes a last look around the park to see that everything is in order. A painter, standing at his easel, tries to capture the gay scene on his canvas. Some young men are attracted by two pretty girls walking with their parents. The painter approaches the older girl and proposes to paint her portrait. She is flattered by his proposal, finding it a great thing to be immortalized. But when the dandy enters, he proves to have precedence over the painter, and the girl goes off with him. Next, a hussar walks by in the company of an entire family. He is courting one of the daughters and is almost too polite to the parents. The hussar and his girl dance a mazurka; then they walk through the park hand in hand.

A group of performers enters. As they prepare to exhibit their art, the barker begins his cry to attract attention to the show. The first to perform is the street dancer. Her solo grows into a *pas de trois* with the barker and the strong man. Suddenly she sees the hussar returning from his walk with the young girl and goes over to him. The young girl shrieks as she discovers that her hussar and the street dancer are old acquaintances. The best thing she thinks she can do in this situation is to faint. Her parents are angry and feel that the hussar is not the right man for their daughter. The jealous street dancer also makes a scene, ending in a faint. The strollers now separate, and the irresolute hussar is left behind with his street dancer. The first bars of the *Blue Danube* waltz are heard. The hussar invites the street dancer to dance, and they execute a *pas de deux*. The girl, in love even though deceived, can not give up her hussar; he is the type of man that women forgive everything. Her love moves the hussar so much that he abandons the street dancer and returns to his girl. In a waltz, he presses his beloved to his heart. The parents, who oppose the match, are won over by the girl's sister, who intercedes for the pair. The parents give their consent. In the finale, everyone dances to celebrate the couple's betrothal.

At the première Massine himself danced the role of the hussar. Alexandra Danilova, the street dancer, and Tatiana Riabouchinska, the daughter, were also highly successful in their roles. The ballet became immediately popular, and it still remains one of the most popular comedy ballets of our time. After the Second World War, Roland Petit and Renée Jeanmaire had great success with it in Europe.

The Rake's Progress

Ballet in six scenes. Book: Gavin Gordon. Choreography: Ninette de Valois. Music: Gavin Gordon. Scenery and costumes: Rex Whistler. Première: May 20, 1935, at the Sadler's Wells Theatre, London, by the Sadler's Wells Ballet.

Characters: rake; tailor; jockey; fencing master; desperado; bugler; dancing master; the betrayed girl; her mother; dancer; servant; rake's friend; ballad singer; musicians; creditors; gamblers; harlots; gentleman with rope; cardplayers; violinist; sailor; the "king"; the "pope"; visitors.

Scene 1. The rake's house.

The curtain rises on a drop curtain, showing a street with many large puddles in the vicinity of Covent Garden. Then the drop curtain rises, revealing the rake's room. The rake is surrounded by people who want to take advantage of his large inheritance. The jockey and then the dancing master dance solos. The tailor takes the rake's measurements for a new suit of clothes. The rake then puts on a handsome rose-red coat. The dancing master shows the rake a few dance steps, and the others leave.

A mother enters the room with her daughter whom the rake has seduced. The rake has lost interest in this dalliance with the daughter, and he now indicates he will have nothing more to do with her. The two women leave, frustrated. The drop curtain falls.

The dancing master appears in front and executes some dance steps. Three women enter from the right. The mother and her daughter also pass through. There is one more passerby. Then the lights go out.

SCENE 2. A house of ill fame.

As the drop curtain goes up, we see a room with a bed that has obviously been slept in. The atmosphere is lascivious. Five very loose and somewhat lively girls come in. A sixth one, the dancer, follows. The rake's friend comes in and does a dance with two of the harlots. Then the rake stumbles in; he can not stay on his feet too well for he has had a lot to drink. He hugs the girls one after the other, and they are delighted. Three of them have a quarrel; two slouch over the table in disreputable postures and look on; one sits under the table. Two musicians enter. One plays the horn, the other a stringed instrument; but the music they produce could never be called pure. The girl ballad singer, who came along with the musicians, stays behind when they leave. A dance by the rake's friend with the five harlots follows. The rake recovers his senses and chases a stocking that one of the girls has taken off. As the curtain falls, everything is in chaos.

SCENE 3. The street.

Three creditors, holding long sheets of paper listing the rake's debts, walk up and down making calculations. The rake appears on the street but turns back when he sees the creditors. The betrayed girl pays the rake's debts. After a long solo, she leaves.

SCENE 4. A gambling den.

Three men are playing dice at a table. The rake, who has had enough of the amusement that the harlots can give him, seeks diversion in the gambling hall. The three men, delighted at this new quarry, plan to lighten the rake's purse for him and begin a card game. Drunk though the rake is, he still sees that the men are trying to cheat him. A fight takes place. Suddenly the rake reaches for his wig and throws it away as the lights go out.

SCENE 5. Near the prison.

The betrayed girl walks around the jail, embroidering as she goes. She dances a very long solo. Then the lights go out.

SCENE 6. The lunatic asylum.

As the curtain rises, we see a hallway in a lunatic asylum. All sorts of patients are lounging around: a card player, a violinist, a sailor, somebody who thinks he is a king, and another who imagines himself to be the pope. They move only slightly or in a monotonous way. The rake enters with the seat of his breeches torn. Then, in turn, each of the patients does a dance. Some visitors enter for a moment. Now the rake starts swinging a rope, and the patients shrink back in terror. The betrayed girl also enters the room. The patients try to take shelter behind each other. The girl dances. Four of the patients gather around her, while the others look on from the left rear. The rake lies down on the floor, exhausted. Three visitors with fans enter and leave. The girl is still dancing. At the sound of a drumbeat the rake gets to his feet and goes all the way to the right. The girl follows him. Four visitors enter. The music becomes shrill. The rake throws his arms around the girl and then falls down in a convulsion, hitting his head; he is dead. The curtain falls.

The Rake's Progress is based on a series of eight paintings by William Hogarth in the Sloane Museum in London. The eight episodes were reduced to six in the ballet by omitting the fifth entirely and by combining the first and second.

The ballet is typical of the beginning of British dance and ballet tradition, for the reason that there is little real dancing. With the exception of the dance solos by the seduced girl and the rake, the ballet is mostly pantomime, and there is no dancing at all in the gambling hall scene. *The Rake's Progress* is still popular in England and appears frequently in repertories. The Sadler's Wells Theatre Ballet also adopted it for their repertory on foreign tours. The roles of the betrayed girl and the rake have been splendidly performed by many British dancers. Cyril Beaumont considers Elizabeth Miller and Robert Helpmann as having been the best interpreters of these roles. At the première the roles were danced by Alicia Markova and Walter Gore.

Jardin aux Lilas ("Lilac Garden")

Ballet in one act. Book: Antony Tudor. Choreography: Antony Tudor. Music: Ernest Chausson (Poème). *Scenery and costumes:*

Hugh Stevenson. Première: January 26, 1936, at the Mercury Theatre, London, by the Ballet Rambert.

CHARACTERS: Caroline; her lover; her fiancé; the woman in the fiancé's past; guests.

❧

The action takes place in the garden of Caroline's home. Lilac bushes are grouped here and there. Caroline, who is soon to be married, is giving a farewell party for her friends. Among the guests are the young man whom she really loves, and, unknown to her, the former mistress of her fiancé.

Caroline is talking with her fiancé. The relationship is obviously conventional; nothing intimate seems to be expressed between them. Then Caroline's lover arrives. The lover is about to go over to Caroline as an ordinary admirer, but is warned off by a silent gesture. Caroline leaves with her fiancé. Her fiancé's mistress enters and dances with Caroline's lover. A little later Caroline returns to meet her lover in the garden but sees only the mistress of her future husband, who does not notice Caroline and who goes off looking for her lover.

Caroline's lover returns, and the pair dance together in tender abandon. Every now and then Caroline interrupts the dance because she is afraid that her fiancé may return. As the couple wander further off in the garden, Caroline's fiancé and his mistress return to the garden. The former sweetheart tries to convince her lover that they can continue to maintain their old relationship. During the quarrel and dance, the fiancé looks around anxiously now and then, for he fears that Caroline may come back and catch him. He thinks it better that Caroline should not know about his former affair. All of this takes place in a series of *pas de deux.*

The ballet ends with a *pas de quatre* of the couples. Caroline has not succeeded in breaking off with her lover, as she had planned, and she leaves the garden on the arm of her future husband.

❧

In this ballet, Antony Tudor has given a splendid example of the expression of drama in dance movements. His inspiration for the work was actually provided by the Finnish writer Aino Kallas. The tale, which Tudor modified substantially, concerned a farm boy and a girl who could not be married until the lord of the manor had exercised his *droit du seigneur*. The girl went to satisfy the lord's demand armed with a dagger.

The original cast included Maude Lloyd, Hugh Laing, Peggy van Praagh, and Antony Tudor. *Jardin aux Lilas* was subsequently accepted for the repertory of Ballet Theatre, Laing and Tudor performing their original roles for many years. Nora Kaye was particularly memorable as Caroline. The ballet was also taken into the repertory (1951) of the New York City Ballet. The National Ballet of Canada performed the work in 1954.

The Prisoner of the Caucasus (II)

Ballet in three acts, a prologue, and seven scenes. Book: Leonid Lavrovsky, N. D. Volkov, and E. S. Zilberstein. Choreography: Leonid Lavrovsky. Music: Boris Asafiev. Scenery: B. M. Khodaze-vich. Première: in 1937 at the Maly Theater, Leningrad.

CHARACTERS: Bakhmetiev; Princess Nina; her father; her cousin; the prince; aide-de-camp; a Circassian girl; a captured officer; the father of the Circassian girl; the fiancé; a horseman; the chief; Circassians; women; musicians.

❧

PROLOGUE, SCENE 1. A hall in a great patrician house in St. Petersburg during the reign of Alexander I.

Guests are assembling for a ball being given by the prince. Bakhmetiev, an Armenian officer dressed in a plain uniform, stands out among the overdecorated guests, who obviously bore him. He has come to see his beloved Nina once more. Four young men ask Bakhmetiev why he has not come in dress uniform, but they soon abandon him because they don't wish anyone important to see them with him.

Princess Nina comes in with her friends, followed by her cousin and her father. She is frightened when she sees Bakhmetiev, to whom she had once given a locket with her portrait. Nina's fiancé, the prince, comes over, and Nina recovers her composure. She introduces the two young men, who bow coldly. The prince leads Nina to the ballroom; Bakhmetiev follows.

PROLOGUE, SCENE 2. The ballroom.

The guests dance a waltz. Nina's cousin is dancing with the aide-de-camp. At the end of the waltz judges choose the cousin to be queen of the cotillion. She receives a ribbon and now must announce the dances at the cotillion. The prince and Nina look on with pleasure.

The "queen" now announces that Princess Nina must dance with the prince and Bakhmetiev. The guests look scornfully at Bakhmetiev; some even leave the ballroom. Nina tries to avoid a quarrel between the two young men. The prince tarries in fulfilling the "queen's" decree, and the situation becomes tense. A group gathers around the prince and opposes Bakhmetiev. At this point the cousin commands Nina to dance alone. During her variation Bakhmetiev leaves the room. Then all dance a waltz.

PROLOGUE, SCENE 3. A drawing room.

Nina enters, sits down on the divan, and starts reading a letter. The prince, who has been looking for her, comes in unexpectedly and takes it from her. At this point Bakhmetiev enters and sees the prince with his letter. The prince folds the note, hands it to its writer, and leaves the room with Nina. Bakhmetiev goes after them, enraged, but is hindered by the other dancers.

PROLOGUE, SCENE 4. Another room.

Bakhmetiev, sunk down on a divan, holds the crumpled letter in his hand. Nina comes in, asks him to forgive her, and begs him to forget her. Bakhmetiev shows her the locket hanging around his neck. She asks him to return the locket, but Bakhmetiev refuses.

Nina's cousin comes in to warn her that the prince is looking for her, whereupon Nina hurriedly leaves the chamber. As the prince comes in, Bakhmetiev throws his glove down before him. The prince bows coldly and proposes his aide-de-camp as his second. Bakhmetiev looks among those present for a second, but everyone turns him down. Nina returns and tries to make peace between the two men. The prince takes Nina by the arm and leaves the room with her.

Bakhmetiev is left alone. Slowly he moves to the window, opens it, and looks out at the swirling snowflakes. To leave St. Petersburg is his only thought.

ACT I. A village in the Caucasus.

Old mountaineers are sitting in front of their huts; one of them tells about times long ago. Women return from the river, where they have filled their jugs. The last to enter is a Circassian girl. She is pensive, because this is the day on which her future husband is to bring the dowry to her father.

Hoofbeats are heard. A richly clad old man comes in on horseback. The father greets him with delight and helps him dismount. The girl realizes that this must be her future husband and can not conceal her dislike. The father leads the guest inside the house.

Now, young men, loaded with booty, come in on horseback. The villagers offer them wine, and soon the young men break into a rapid dance. The Circassian girl's fiancé joins the dancers, and at her father's command the daughter dances briefly with her betrothed. Then she escapes into her hut. The dancing continues until shots signaling another victory are heard.

A young horseman trots up with a Russian officer whom he has taken prisoner. The villagers insult the prisoner and put him in chains, and the horseman swears vengeance on all Russians. The women look at the officer with curiosity. Thinking his exploit has pleased the young girl, the horseman starts to declare his love to her, but her betrothed appears. In order to avoid a fight between the rivals, the girls begin a dance. The young horseman outdoes himself in the dance to attract the maid's attention, but her interest has been only in the captured officer. The horseman asks for her hand, and then her betrothed asks for an answer to his proposal of marriage. Suddenly realizing what is expected of her, the girl runs into her hut.

The horseman calls the young men together for a new attack on the Russians. They answer the call and go off to another battle.

Quiet returns to the village. The prisoner is left alone. Night falls. The girl comes out of her cabin, goes over to the prisoner, washes his face, and tries to comfort him.

ACT II. The following day.

The prisoner sits disconsolately, thinking of his lost freedom. A locket falls from his neck; he picks it up and presses it to his heart tenderly. Several visions of Nina follow, then slowly fade away.

The Circassian girl comes in with food, sits down near the Russian officer, and confesses her love for him. Then she sees the locket, opens it, and asks who the girl is. The officer tells her of

St. Petersburg and his love for Nina. The girl, dismayed, realizes that he can not love her.

Act III. Daybreak.

The prisoner looks around; the surroundings remind him of his own country. Voices of mountaineers are heard; preparations are in progress for a new attack. Nearby, young men amuse themselves by playing war; they come nearer and menace the captured officer. Then a *lezghinka* is danced by all.

Now the leaders form the plans for their operation, and all leave. The prisoner makes futile efforts to free himself and finally falls down exhausted.

The girl enters with a file and a dagger. Perhaps if she frees the prisoner he can love her. But he says he never could love her; nevertheless, she continues filing his chains.

Cossack songs are heard in the distance. When the prisoner hears them, he runs toward the mountains, overjoyed. Then he looks back and sees the girl's sad face. He stops, returns, and proposes that they run away together. The girl points to the locket. Joyful over this freedom, the officer throws the locket to the ground, but the girl still declines. He then throws the locket into the river and declares his love. He tries once more to persuade her to go with him, but she is afraid that she could not be happy in a strange land and persists in her refusal. His longing for his people is too great for him to stay with the girl, so the officer departs. The Circassian girl accompanies him as far as the mountains and gazes after him until he has disappeared from sight; then she flings herself into the roaring stream below.

This Russian version is closer to the original poem by Pushkin than was the nineteenth-century ballet choreographed by Charles Didelot (see p. 22). Naturally it omitted the technical tricks with wires that were prominent in the earlier version. And it is notable for Lavrosky's excellent use of typical Caucasian folk dances—both for men and for women.

In a version altered somewhat by Rostislav Zakharov, *The Prisoner of the Caucasus* was given in Moscow on August 17, 1938, in an open-air theater seating 20,000 persons. Here the ballet began with Act I (in the mountain village), whereas portions of the prologue were shown in Act II as the officer told the Circassian girl about his life and love in St. Petersburg. Act III was similar to that shown in Leningrad.

The production on this occasion was an outstanding example of the Russian conception that a ballet must be a genuine theater work. The Circassian riders actually came in on horseback; even dogs and cattle appeared on stage. The entire cast, including members of the orchestra, numbered five hundred. The organization required to put on a work with such a large cast, the time required for rehearsals, and the financial resources necessary for costumes and wages could hardly be equaled anywhere else in the world. If we then add the splendid Russian ballet training and the arsenal of folk dance that the choreographer can draw upon, we can achieve some idea of the impression that such a performance must make on a spectator.

Another version of *The Prisoner of the Caucasus,* choreographed by George Skibine, deserves special mention. The première took place on December 4, 1951, at the Empire Theater, Paris, performed by the Marquis de Cuevas Ballet. This production was especially commissioned to use some lavish sets and costumes that had come into the possession of the Marquis de Cuevas: those for Ballet International's 1944 production of *Prince Goudal.** Skibine was particularly successful in creating a work for the theater alternating folk dances, pantomime, and classical ballet—although the latter in the second scene is not entirely logical. Skibine followed closely Pushkin's poem and had the ballet begin with the battle near the Circassian camp. The principals at the première were Marjorie Tallchief, George Skibine, and Oleg Sabline. Delores Starr and Daniel Selier were a sensation in their striking short duet as two of the younger Circassians in the second scene.

* Since ballet productions are very expensive to mount and so many companies work on limited budgets, it is not unusual for choreographers to be commissioned to create ballets for which costumes and sets available from a previous, unsuccessful ballet can be used.

Billy the Kid

Ballet in eleven episodes. Book: Lincoln Kirstein. Choreography: Eugene Loring. Music: Aaron Copland. Scenery and costumes: Jared French. Premiére: October 16, 1938, at the Chicago Opera House, by Ballet Caravan.

CHARACTERS: Billy; his friend, Sheriff Pat Garrett; Alias; Billy's mother; warden; postman; professional dancing girls; cowboy in red; Mexican girls; Billy's Mexican sweetheart; women; cowgirls in gray and cowgirls in light brown; cowboys.

❧

EPISODE 1. American pioneers are going west. Men and women—in pairs, and finally in threes—pass from left to right slowly across a bare landscape dotted with cacti in the background.

EPISODE 2. There is a street crowded with girls, a mailman, and a few professional dancing girls with plumes and boots. Men enter, their movements indicating they are riding on horseback; they execute a dance together. Each of the girls manages to find a partner. Billy appears in the street with his mother. Where everything seemed to be so pleasant, a quarrel suddenly breaks out—between Alias and a cowboy—over one of the dancing girls. Billy tries to part them, but his mother holds him back. Alias fires at his adversary, but the shot hits Billy's mother instead. She falls. Billy hesitates but a moment before stabbing Alias to death. Then he escapes. The bystanders stand motionless for a moment. Then one of the young men lifts up the body of Billy's mother and another picks up Alias. Everyone exits.

EPISODE 3. Billy enters the empty stage. Someone passes by. Billy is again left alone. In a solo he expresses his feeling of being lonesome, frightened, and hunted, but the dance ends with an outburst of rebellion.

EPISODE 4. Alias (the foreman) appears with two men looking for the outlaw Billy. Billy quickly hides. As the three men are about to leave, Billy takes advantage of the opportunity to kill Alias with a well-aimed shot.

EPISODE 5. Billy is playing cards with his friend Pat Garrett, the sheriff. Cowboys and cowgirls come in. Pat catches Billy cheating. After a quarrel with Billy over the cards, Pat finally rides off. The music becomes louder, heralding misfortune.

EPISODE 6. Pat returns with a posse. Two groups are formed. Pat Garrett, Alias (the deputy sheriff), and citizens oppose Billy and his band. Girls as well as young men take part in a wild gunfight. Finally Billy is captured. He is taken off to jail, but not before he has killed Alias. The posse celebrates Billy's capture. Billy's Mexican sweetheart, who has been searching for Billy, enters.

EPISODE 7. Billy passes time in his cell by playing cards with Alias (the warden). Through a trick Billy manages to get the warden's gun. Billy shoots Alias dead; he is free.

EPISODE 8. A posse looking for Billy enters, and the outlaw hides behind some Mexican girls. Then he escapes on horseback, with the help of Alias (an Indian guide).

EPISODE 9. Billy is alone; night falls. He removes his excess clothing. Behind Billy, we see the dancing dream figure of the girl he loves. At one point she touches him, and he gets up and dances a *pas de deux* with her. The girl then dances away.

Billy is restless; there is danger everywhere. Finally he lies down to get the sleep he needs so much. Alias the guide, who has meanwhile betrayed Billy, returns with Pat Garrett. Billy is awakened from his light sleep by a sound. Did he hear anything? He gets up nervously and calls out, "¿Quién es?" (Who is it?). Everything is still. Billy sighs in relief and lights a cigarette. There is a shot, and Billy falls, mortally wounded. Garrett, his best friend, has killed him in the line of duty.

EPISODE 10. Mourning women pass by. Although Billy was an outlaw, he was loved by many women.

EPISODE 11. American pioneers are journeying westward, pushing back the frontier.

The subject of *Billy the Kid* was taken from the life story of William Bonney, who was born in New York in 1859 and went west with his mother when a child. The unlucky shot that killed his mother was one reason that he became a desperado.

Many people regard *Billy the Kid* as the first important American ballet. The staging is excellent; the subject rather dramatic.

The dance, based on the movements of horsemen, belongs more or less to an expressionistic school.

At the première, the roles of Billy, Pat Garrett, sweetheart-mother (double role), and Alias were taken by Eugene Loring, Lew Christensen, Marie-Jeanne, and Todd Bolender, respectively. American Ballet Theatre first performed the work in 1940, and it has appeared intermittently in the repertory of the company ever since, with John Kriza in the role of Billy.

Romeo and Juliet

Ballet in three acts, thirteen scenes, with a prologue and epilogue. Book: Leonid Lavrovsky, Serge Prokofiev, and Serge Radlov. Music: Serge Prokofiev. Choreography: Leonid Lavrovsky. Scenery: Peter Williams. Première: January 11, 1940, at the Kirov State Theater, Leningrad.

CHARACTERS: Prince of Verona; Paris, a young nobleman; his page; Romeo; his father, Montague; Juliet; her parents, the Capulets; Mercutio, a friend of Romeo; Benvolio, Romeo's cousin and friend; Tybalt, a cousin of Lady Capulet; Friar Lawrence; Friar John; Balthasar, Romeo's servant; Samson, Gregory, and Peter, servants in the house of Capulet; Juliet's nurse and her servant; Abraham, a servant of Montague; landlord; maidservants; friends of Juliet; troubadours; two beggar children; a jester with four companions; street vendors; pages; retinue of the Capulet family; crowd.

As the music begins, the curtain goes up revealing a drop curtain with stylized flowers and shrubs bathed in a red light. Then the drop curtain is raised.

PROLOGUE. Romeo, Juliet, and Friar Lawrence stand motionless in front of three arches.

ACT I, SCENE 1. A square in Verona in the early morning. To the left is a house with a large statue a few yards in front of it. To the right, a short flight of stairs leads to a bridge. Also on the right is a large gate.

The last revelers and the first merchants pass through the square. Romeo, unable to sleep, walks across the square. A priest hurries to early mass. A market woman removes her wares from a boat. Servant girls enter and straighten out the chairs in front of the tavern. Gregory, Peter, and Samson, servants in the house of Capulet, enter and go over to the girls in order to have some fun with them. Two servants of the Montague family, Balthasar and Abraham, come in. The Capulet servants take a dim view of the appearance of their colleagues, and start to test their strength against them. Abraham and Balthasar bar the way, and the affair ends with a sword fight. Benvolio comes in just in time to see one of the men wounded. He orders them to put away their swords, and the servants of the house of Capulet leave. Then Tybalt appears and insults Benvolio, and another fight breaks out. Paris enters; he is on his way to the house of Capulet to ask for Juliet's hand. Capulet himself then emerges from his house to take part in the fight. The noise awakens the people of Verona, so that finally the prince himself comes out with his guard to restore order. He commands that the swords be put away and proclaims that thereafter possession of arms will be punished by death. The crowd breaks up. Tybalt and his friends leave, cursing the Montagues; the wounded man is carried off to the right. The drop curtain falls.

ACT I, SCENE 2. Juliet and her nurse dance along in front of the drop curtain, followed by two servants. One of them carries a large jug, the other a stool. The nurse chases the servants away.

The drop curtain rises to disclose Juliet's room. In the room at the left is a large wardrobe with a mirror; an adjacent curtain conceals the balcony. In the center rear is an armchair; behind it hangs a life-sized portrait of a woman; to the right, a four-poster and a bay window. The wall is covered with tapestries.

Juliet and the nurse entertain each other. Their conversation is interrupted by the arrival of Juliet's mother, who sits down in the armchair; Juliet's nurse sits next to her on the floor. The mother informs Juliet that Paris has asked her hand in marriage. Juliet thinks that she is still too young, but her mother shows her in the mirror that she really has reached a marriageable age. Juliet seems a little perplexed at this. The drop curtain falls.

A number of servants with trays containing the dishes for the feast of the Capulet family pass before the drop curtain.

ACT I, SCENE 3. The drop curtain rises on a great hall that leads to the ballroom. The background is filled by a wall tapestry. Large candelabras stand along the side wall; some columns are in the middle. (The same setting, but without the columns, is later used for the ballroom.)

Richly attired guests enter the hall. A troubadour and Juliet's bosom friend enter. They are alone for a moment and take advantage of the opportunity to dance a short duet. New guests arrive: six of Juliet's friends, followed by six troubadours. They, too, dance briefly before entering the ballroom. The guests keep streaming in; Paris, with his page, brings up the rear. The drop curtain falls.

Servants carrying lamps pass in front of the drop curtain. Mercutio and Benvolio come in, followed by Romeo, who is wrapped in a black cape. Romeo's friends urge him to accompany them to the Capulet feast. After a little hesitation he consents, puts on a domino mask, takes a lamp from a servant, and goes with his friends to the ball. The drop curtain rises.

ACT I, SCENE 4. The ballroom of the Capulets.

The hall is filled with guests, perhaps about eighty in number. Juliet is sitting on a bench near the front. Her father and mother enter the hall. Paris gives his beloved a bouquet of roses. Juliet takes the nosegay and goes to the back of the hall, where there is a large table. The guests form in groups along the sides of the hall. The ball begins with a formal dance. The men lay cushions at the feet of the women, kneel down on them, and kiss the hems of the ladies' skirts. The men then execute a dance. After the women take the cushions and do a dance in one figure of which they hold the cushions above their heads, there is a dance in which the pairs stride slowly and stately. Finally, the cushions are placed on the ground, and both men and women kneel on one knee and embrace. During the dance Juliet remains at the table with her nurse and friends and arranges the flowers. After the dance she rises and goes to the center of the room to perform a wonderfully light dance. She stops suddenly and returns to the table, and the dance of the couples resumes. Then Juliet comes to the fore again and dances a longer solo. At this moment Romeo and his friends enter the hall. Romeo, enraptured, goes over to Juliet, but Paris comes between them. The guests go to the side. Mercutio tries

to get the attention of the guests by jesting and takes the opportunity to execute a long solo. The troubadours then leave, followed
by Mercutio and Benvolio. Juliet also starts to leave but changes
her mind and stays to dance a long *pas de deux* with Romeo,
at the end of which the drop curtain falls in a curve, so that we
have a sidelong view of the ballroom.

Juliet and Romeo are in front of the drop curtain. Romeo's
mask falls off, and Juliet finds that he is a handsome young man
whom she thinks she could love. At this moment Tybalt appears.
He thinks that he recognizes the young man as Romeo, the enemy
of the house of Capulet, and hurries off to tell Juliet's father, who
arrives at that moment. Romeo quickly puts on his mask. Tybalt
tries to attack Romeo but is held back by Mercutio and finally
sent away by Juliet's father. For an instant Romeo plays hide-and-
seek with Juliet around the low-hanging curtain, and then the drop
curtain goes up.

The ball is still going on. There are dances by Juliet and her
friends, by the troubadour, and by the troubadour and Juliet's
bosom friend. Then all dance, and the drop curtain again comes
down in a curve.

Four servants pass by with candelabras. The feast is over, and
the guests are going home. Juliet, in a black cape, stands at the
left and learns from her nurse that the handsome youth is Romeo
Montague.

ACT I, SCENE 5. The garden in front of Juliet's house. Moonlight.

Juliet, thinking of Romeo, dances through the garden like a
ghost. Romeo comes in from the left. As the light gets brighter,
the two lovers do a long *pas de deux* of love, a *pas de deux* that is
enchanting more for its expressiveness than for its choreography.
It ends with a passionate embrace.

ACT II, SCENE 1. A square. Right, a large building and a
tavern. Center rear, some arches. In the distance, mountains. Above
the center of the stage, a balustrade and behind it a path leading
upwards. Left, a gateway.

A gay crowd of people is celebrating. Eighteen couples do a
series of stylized folk dances; the boys and girls dance by turns,
followed by a solo of one of the waitresses, later joined by the two
other waitresses in a kind of *pas de trois*. In the meantime the
proprietor is very busy with the guests. Then a procession with an

image of the Madonna comes in from the left and marches across the stage, stopping where a jester executes a solo with complicated acrobatic leaps. Benvolio and Mercutio are sitting in the café and flirting with the women. They take the waitresses by the hand and do a dance, and then the whole crowd dances. Juliet's nurse appears, looking for Romeo. Mercutio mocks her for being fat. Romeo comes into the square; she sees him and whispers something into his ear. The drop curtain falls.

In front of the drop curtain the nurse meets Romeo. She has a letter for him from Juliet. When Romeo, curious, tries to take the letter, she puts it back teasingly, but finally hands it to him. In the letter Juliet tells Romeo that she will marry him.

ACT II, SCENE 2. Friar Lawrence's cell. In the cell are a table with a skull and some flowers, a chair, and, on the floor, a basket of flowers. To the left is a bust of the Virgin and Child.

Lawrence is contemplating the skull and flowers. Romeo enters with Juliet's letter and kneels down before him. Then he rises and takes first one flower, then another; when finally he takes the skull, he drops the flowers. Soon Juliet, wearing a black cape, enters. Friar Lawrence kneels before the image of the Virgin, then rises and unites Romeo and Juliet in marriage. He kneels down again before the Virgin, and, after a tender embrace by Romeo and Juliet, the drop curtain falls.

The jester and his companions dance in front of the drop curtain. Six couples come along, then beggar children, a fruit vendor, Tybalt, Capulet, and a procession of people. Mercutio, in high spirits, buys all the vendor's fruit and distributes the contents to the girls around. Tybalt becomes enraged when someone accidentally touches him. The drop curtain rises.

ACT II, SCENE 3. The square in Verona.

The festival continues. Sixteen couples dance with tambourines. Two additional pairs dance. Mercutio dances with the waitresses. Tybalt comes in, see Mercutio, and challenges him to a duel. Romeo enters and tries to make peace, but Tybalt laughs mockingly at him. Mercutio goes back to the table in front of the café, but Tybalt continues to challenge him. The duel begins. Mercutio does well. But unfortunately he looks at Romeo for an unguarded instant, and Tybalt makes a deadly thrust. Tybalt leaves laughing, as Mercutio totters. In a long solo the young Mercutio struggles against death. Finally he drops his sword and falls. The crowd bows its head. Romeo bends over his friend to listen for a heartbeat, but there is none. Mercutio is carried off. Romeo, about to follow, looks around and sees Tybalt swaggering back onto the square. The sight is too much for him. He draws his sword and rushes up the stairs at Tybalt. In the struggle, Romeo is the stronger; he wounds Tybalt fatally. Romeo escapes. Juliet's father, mother, and nurse come out of the house. The nurse orders servants to bring a bier. Juliet's mother is so grieved over the loss of her cousin that she kneels down next to him on the bier. Tybalt is carried off. Everyone in the square kneels down. The curtain falls.

ACT III, SCENE 1. The curtain rises on the drop curtain, illuminated by an orange light. After a short pause the drop curtain goes up revealing Juliet's bedchamber. In the left foreground is a large mirrored wardrobe; next to it is a curtain, behind which is a balcony. In the center rear is a large armchair; at the right is a four-poster. Juliet is on the bed. Romeo is at her feet.

The lovers are deep in caresses. Romeo stands up after a few moments, opens the curtain to the balcony, and looks out. It is already daylight. Juliet quickly draws the curtain again. A long *pas de deux* of love follows. Then Juliet thinks she hears a sound. The household is waking up; Romeo must leave. After a parting kiss, Romeo disappears by way of the balcony.

Juliet's nurse enters, followed by Juliet's mother, father, and Paris. Paris bows down to kiss the hem of Juliet's dress, but she draws back. He tries to kiss her hand, but she avoids that mark of respect, too, and Paris goes off, hurt and resentful. Juliet turns to her parents and tells them that she does not want to marry Paris. There is an argument; Juliet's mother and nurse leave the room. The father scuffles with Juliet, who falls down. He leaves the room. Juliet dances a solo of despair. Finally she takes her cape and runs out. The drop curtain falls. Juliet runs across the stage.

ACT III, SCENE 2. The music continues without interruption as the stage is briefly empty. Finally, the drop curtain rises on the cell of Friar Lawrence.

Juliet, distraught, comes in and drops into a chair by the table; she jumps up and then falls down before the image of the Madonna. Friar Lawrence goes to his table and takes a small object from a chest. Juliet rises, notices a dagger on the table, and snatches it, but Friar Lawrence takes the weapon away from her and shows her a small object, a vial with a sleeping potion. If she takes the contents of the flask, people will think that she is dead. Juliet gladly accepts the vial. The drop curtain comes down, leaving only a small opening through which Juliet leaves. Friar Lawrence watches her go, and then closes the drop curtain.

Act III, Scene 3. Juliet's bedchamber.

In the room are Capulet, Lady Capulet, Paris, and Juliet's nurse. Juliet enters in her black cape. She hesitates for an instant, then goes out on the balcony. On re-entering the room, she consents to a marriage with Paris. Paris comes up to her, takes the cape from her shoulders, and hands it to the nurse. Then he and Juliet dance a *pas de deux*. Her parents leave, joyful and contented. The nurse displays the wedding gown; then she, too, leaves. Paris goes over to Juliet, but she holds herself aloof; he leaves the room uncertainly. Juliet goes over to her bridal dress, touches it, then gazes at the garden. The moment has come for her to take Friar Lawrence's potion. In a long solo she expresses the difficulty of deciding to swallow the potion. Finally she drinks the contents of the vial and falls down on the bed. A curtain falls in front of the bed, leaving the rest of the room visible. It is morning. Juliet's bosom friend comes in with flowers, followed by a troubadour. Her other friends come in with the other troubadours; there is a dance. Then, with Juliet's nurse at his heels, Paris enters to fetch his bride. But the wedding dress is on the chair; Juliet must still be asleep! Paris wants to look behind the curtain, but the nurse stops him. Juliet's father and mother enter the room and tell the nurse to wake her up. The nurse shrinks back from the curtain with a shriek. The curtain now goes up, revealing Juliet lying on her bed. Everyone breaks into sobs. The drop curtain comes down and is suffused with purple light.

Act III, Scene 4. The music continues, and the drop curtain rises, showing a street in Mantua.

Romeo, wandering around disconsolately, expresses his wretchedness in a long solo. Finally his servant Balthasar arrives from Verona and tells him that Juliet is dead. Balthasar puts his cape around Romeo. The drop curtain falls.

Romeo, in front of the drop curtain, hesitates for a few moments; then with a gesture of determination, he hurries off.

Act III, Scene 5. The burial vault in Verona.

A procession of mourners comes in with Juliet's body, which is placed on a tomb at the top of the flight of steps. Paris runs up the steps and kneels before the bier. The others lie on the floor or support each other in their grief. After Paris has gone, darkness falls over the tomb; only Juliet's bier is illuminated. Everyone leaves the vault.

Romeo rushes in. He runs up the steps and kneels before Juliet; he then draws the veil back from her face, kisses her, and takes her in his arms. He carries her down the steps and holds her on his knees. Then he picks her up and ascends the steps, holding Juliet over his head on one hand, to set her back on her tomb. Romeo puts her down gently, takes poison, and dies, falling backward down the steps. After a few moments the effect of the sleeping potion having worn off, Juliet awakes. She sits up and is happy to see Romeo. She descends from her bier, and bends over and caresses him. But Romeo is dead. Juliet does not falter; she takes Romeo's dagger, stabs herself, and falls backward across the body of her beloved.

EPILOGUE. Juliet's parents, Paris, and Montague enter, followed by a crowd. The two fathers take each other's hand over the bodies of their dead children as the crowd kneels.

Romeo and Juliet has inspired a number of choreographers. The best-known of the resultant dramatic ballets is that here described, the choreography of Leonid Lavrovsky for the Bolshoi Ballet. Prokofiev's music was composed in close collaboration with the choreographer. This *Romeo and Juliet,* which follows Shakespeare's text fairly closely, is a full-length work, in which pantomime plays a great role. There are even lip movements, when they are considered necessary! Lavrovsky, not content with imitative gestures, demands complete understanding of the role. In dramatic ballet Lavrovsky believes either the dance must emerge naturally from the pantomimed and mimed action, or the pantomimed action must be a logical part of the dance. In general, Lavrovsky has succeeded in his task. Only those scenes in which despair is expressed by pirouettes and *grand jetés* remain incomprehensible. At the première Galina Ulanova was enthusiastically applauded in the role of Juliet, and the part of Romeo was danced by Konstantin Sergeyev and was later taken over by Yuri Zhdanov.

Many ballets have been inspired by *Romeo and Juliet*. Among them were two early works: a ballet choreographed by Eusebio Luzzi in 1785, and a work produced in Copenhagen on April 2, 1811, with choreography by Vincenzo Galeotti and Antoine Bournonville and music by Klaus Schall. After these two ballets, the story was confined to the dramatic stage until May 4, 1926, when, at Monte Carlo, Bronislava Nijinska presented a version with music by Constant Lambert; Serge Lifar and Thamar Karsavina danced the lovers. In 1939 Gyula Harangozó offered a version of *Romeo and Juliet* to Tchaikovsky's music at the Budapest Opera. Antony Tudor presented a version on April 6, 1942, with Ballet Theatre; Alicia Markova and Hugh Laing took the title parts, and the music comprised several pieces by Frederick Delius. At Monte Carlo, in 1946, a *Romeo and Juliet* choreographed by Serge Lifar to music by Tchaikovsky was given; this version was later adopted by both the Paris Opéra and the Marquis de Cuevas Ballet (1950). The Marquis de Cuevas company presented a second version of the Romeo and Juliet story the same year it added the Lifar work to its repertory. George Skibine's *Tragedy at Verona*, also set to music by Tchaikovsky, was first performed on August 4, 1950. Yet another work to Tchaikovsky's music was that by the choreographer Birger Bartholin (1900–   ) which had its première in Copenhagen on December 8, 1950. The London Festival Ballet, under the artistic direction of Anton Dolin, also used Tchaikovsky's music for its production, first shown at the Royal Festival Hall, London, on August 27, 1958; choreography was by Oleg Briansky; scenery and costumes were by the French designer André Levasseur; and Nathalie Krassovska and Briansky danced the principal roles.

The majority of the other ballets based on this story have been set to Prokofiev's score. These include a version by Dmitri Parlic (1917–   ), first performed at Belgrade on June 25,

1948 (and a disappointment when shown in Holland in 1958); a rival version by Margarita Froman, which had its première at Zagreb in June, 1949; a work by the British choreographer Frederick Ashton for the Royal Danish Ballet, first presented in Copenhagen on May 19, 1955; another Lifar treatment, first given in December, 1955; a work by Boris Pilato, given at Bonn, Germany, during the 1955–56 season; and a *Romeo e Guilietta* by the British choreographer John Cranko, presented in Italy during the summer of 1958, with scenery and costumes by Nicola Benois.

To this continuous flow of *Romeo and Juliet* ballets there must be added the ballet set to the music of Hector Berlioz. This *Romeo* was produced in the Cour Carré of the Louvre, Paris, on June 28, 1955, by the Marquis de Cuevas Ballet. The choreography was created by George Skibine, John Taras, Vladimir Skuratoff, and Serge Golovine. The costumes were designed after Léonor Fini, and the scenery was by François Ganeau.

The subject also inspired Jerome Robbins, but in an entirely different way. The musical *West Side Story,* which Robbins directed and choreographed, was the success of the 1957–58 New York season. Two adolescent gangs, one of Puerto Ricans in corduroy jackets and the other of Irish and Italian West Siders in blue jeans, are led by Bernardo the Shark (Tybalt) and Riff the Jet (Mercutio), respectively. Fourteen-year-old Maria (Juliet) of Bernardo's gang is the love of Rony (Romeo) of the Jets. A street fight, a duel, and a climb up a drainpipe to Maria's fire escape are contemporary realizations of events in Shakespeare's drama. It is not "*Hamlet* in evening dress" but "*Romeo and Juliet* in ponytails and blue jeans in the New York slums." Who but Robbins could make such a thing succeed? According to the American critics, *West Side Story* was a turning point in the style of musicals. The score was by Leonard Bernstein, the book by Arthur Laurento, lyrics by Stephen Sondheim, costumes by Irene Sharaff, lighting by Jean Rosenthal, and scenery by Oliver Smith.

Graduation Ball

Ballet in one act. Book and choreography: David Lichine. Music: Johann Strauss, orchestrated by Antal Dorati. Scenery and costumes: Alexandre Benois. Première: February 28, 1940, at the Royal Theatre, Sydney, Australia, by the Original Ballet Russe.

CHARACTERS: headmistress of a girls' boarding school (sometimes danced by a man); first pupil; second pupil; old general; first cadet; drummer; boarding school girls; cadets.

The headmistress of a girls' boarding school in Vienna in the Victorian period has invited a number of cadets to the graduation ball. The older pupils are busily engaged in the preparations for the ball; the younger ones, less serious, are enjoying themselves. When everything is in order, the old general and his cadets march in. The girls and the principal are very curious. The first encounters between the boys and girls do not go too smoothly, but gradually the young people relax a bit, and the dance begins. There is a series of *divertissements* (by the drummer, a sylph, and a Scotsman) for the amusement of those present. There is also an impromptu, a competition in dance steps, a perpetual motion by three girls, and finally a flirtation (mazurka by the old general and the headmistress).

The general and the headmistress now feel that the time has come to give the young people a little more freedom, and they disappear for a while, returning just in time to prevent the jollity from getting out of hand. The well-known game of musical chairs follows, with the general and the headmistress happily looking on. After a gay waltz the party comes to an end. The girls give the boys their hair ribbons as keepsakes. The general and the cadets march off; the principal and the girls wave good-by. Night falls, and the girls go off to bed. One of the cadets and one of the girls return to the party room, obviously with a romantic interest in each other. The general, searching for the deserter, collides with the headmistress, who has discovered the escape of her charge. They collar the fugitives and take them off. Order is restored.

At the première, the main roles were danced by Borislav Runanine (headmistress), Igor Schwezoff (old general), David Lichine (first cadet), Nicholas Orloff (drummer), and Tatiana Riabouchinska (first pupil).

The American Ballet Theatre presented a version of the ballet on October 8, 1944, with Lichine and Riabouchinska repeating their performances of the principal roles. Others in the cast were John Kriza, Rosella Hightower, Alicia Alonso, Richard Reed, Harold Lang, and Marjorie Tallchief. The sylph-Scotsman *pas de deux* was replaced by a classic *pas de deux* (for Alonso and Reed), and a Tyrolean dance was added (for Lang).

Graduation Ball, a gay, airy work is eminently suited as a closing ballet and has been a good, box-office attraction. Lichine has been busy in recent years rehearsing the work for various ballet companies.

Pillar of Fire

Ballet in one act. Book and choreography: Antony Tudor. Music: Arnold Schönberg's Verklärte Nacht. *Scenery and costumes: Jo Mielziner. Première: April 8, 1942, at the Metropolitan Opera House, New York, by Ballet Theatre.*

CHARACTERS: Hagar; the oldest sister; the youngest sister; the friend; the young man from the house opposite; lovers-in-experience; lovers-in-innocence; maiden ladies out walking.

The curtain goes up, revealing an imposing house on the right, with a few steps leading up to the door; left, a less imposing house with one door and one window, from which a light shines through half-closed shutters.

Hagar is at the right, not far from her house. The oldest sister comes home and goes inside. A girl comes by with two boys. Hagar goes to the house opposite and tries to look in through the shutters; then she retraces her steps. A self-conscious young man in a bright pink waistcoat comes out of the shuttered house. When he sees Hagar, he takes off his jacket and leaves. A number of boys and girls do a simple dance. Hagar leans against a doorpost and finally sits down on the stoop. The youngest sister comes out of the house with a young man, who will later prove to be Hagar's friend. The group of dancing boys and girls goes into the background. Hagar goes over to her friend and her sister, but this pair too disappears, so that Hagar is left alone. The group of young people again pass by.

The youngest sister enters again with the friend. As if by accident she pushes the friend toward Hagar, who then falls eagerly into his arms. But thereafter the youngest sister disappears again with the friend. The young man with the pink waistcoat enters from the house opposite. Three flighty girls follow at his heels. Hagar's insecurity is thoroughly revealed in a *pas de deux* with the man in the pink waistcoat. When the girls are gone, Hagar follows the young man into the house opposite. After a few moments she comes out, a ruined woman. The house opposite disappears from the stage.

The oldest sister comes out of the house and looks with scorn at Hagar, who stands with her head bowed. Two ladies come along. The oldest sister does not conceal her disapproval of her sister's behavior and shakes her fist threateningly. Hagar sinks to the ground, deeply miserable. The oldest sister pulls her up roughly. The young man to whom Hagar had yielded passes by. Others come by refusing to recognize her. The youngest sister enters with the friend and goes inside. Hagar tries to hold fast to the friend, but in vain. The door closes; the stage darkens.

The light grows brighter, and a moonlit forest can be discerned. The three sisters enter. Hagar falls on her knees. Boys and girls enter and dance around the fallen Hagar. After the two sisters have gone away, the young people go off too. Hagar stumbles around in desperation. Finally, her friend enters. He puts his arm around her waist. Hagar weeps. In a long *pas de deux,* the friend tries to embrace her. But Hagar is ashamed and draws back. Finally she gives in.

As the young people come up, the friend disappears. The seducer passes by once more. He shows little interest in Hagar and rejects her advances. She sinks to the ground.

The youngest sister goes through some dance steps with the seducer, who has returned. They go off, and Hagar is left to her fate again. The betrayer appears once more, but only for a brief moment—to emphasize Hagar's loneliness.

After a short time the friend and the young people return. The young people indicate their disapproval. Hagar reacts by dancing a long solo in which she expresses her despair. The oldest sister returns, and Hagar seeks understanding of her actions, but everyone remains motionless. The friend enters, and fortunately turns out to be forgiving. A long *pas de deux* of love follows. At the end of this *pas de deux,* the two sink down together in the forest. Young people, the sisters, and ladies pass by. The lovers find each other in a tender embrace.

❦

Arnold Schönberg composed *Verklärte Nacht* around 1900 as an instrumental sextet; later, he reworked the piece for string orchestra. On the score he cited verses of a poem by Richard Dehmel, a German philosopher and poet of that time. In Dehmel's poem a woman who has lost faith in happiness gives herself in despair to a man who does not love her, but when a man who does love her finds out that she is going to have a child that is not his, he accepts her nonetheless. In Tudor's dance drama there is an impression that the woman takes too long in deciding which man to prefer—perhaps because she is repeatedly rejected by the friend.

At the première Lucia Chase, co-director of American Ballet Theatre, appeared as the oldest sister, a role she danced for many years thereafter. Nora Kaye achieved a brilliant success as Hagar; Annabelle Lyon interpreted the youngest sister; Hugh Laing, the young man; and Antony Tudor, the friend.

Rodeo

Ballet in two scenes. Book and choreography: Agnes de Mille. Music: Aaron Copland. Scenery: Oliver Smith. Costumes: Kermit Love. Première: October 16, 1942, at the Metropolitan Opera House, New York, by the Ballet Russe de Monte Carlo.

CHARACTERS: the head wrangler; champion roper; cowgirl; rancher's daughter; her friends, girls from Kansas City; square-dance caller; local girls.

SCENE 1. A corral where a Saturday afternoon rodeo is being held.

Eight cowboys enter, followed by a cowgirl wearing clothing identical to that of the men: shirt, riding pants, boots, cowboy hat. The only thing different about the girl is a couple of small braids. The men do a dance, which creates the illusion that they are on horseback doing typical rodeo stunts and tricks. The girl refuses to be outdone and competes with them. Now the rancher's daughter and her friends from Kansas City arrive and have fun watching the contests and exhibitions. The rancher's daughter takes a fancy to the head wrangler and begins to flirt with him. The cowgirl, angry and disgusted because she too is partial to the head wrangler, petulantly leaves but soon returns astride a bucking bronco. This last attempt at showing off leads to her disgrace, for she is finally thrown from the bronco. The rancher's daughter and her friends, taken aback by the cowgirl's actions, laugh heartily when she falls. Five of the young men do a dance, which the cowgirl joins in an attempt to regain her camaraderie with them, but the head wrangler orders her to leave. The rodeo is over, and the young men start home; the girls wave good-by.

It is evening. Girls and boys walk around in groups. They begin to choose partners; the cowgirl goes over to the head wrangler. Another girl is already there. Finally everybody has a partner except the cowgirl. Vexed, she tries to figure out the cause of her failure. A young man comes over to her, but she turns him away. Couples pass by in the background, and the cowgirl sinks down sadly.

In an interlude in front of a curtain, on which are represented a number of horses appearing to fly through the air, square dancers do the Appalachian running square dance. A number of figures are executed at a tempo somewhat faster than is usual in square dances.

SCENE 2. A large room in the ranch house. Because the room has no roof, a large expanse of night sky can be seen. On the left are some pictures on the wall, and on the right are a stove, a window, and some racks with plates. In the center is a door, where the lonely cowgirl is sitting on a bench.

Several couples come in and dance a 1900 dance to a sort of pianola music. A cowhand goes over to the cowgirl, but leaves her immediately to chase after a flirtatious girl looking for a partner. Fortunately the roper arrives. He picks up the cowgirl rather roughly, straightens her clothes out a little, dusts her off, and is just about to dance with her when the wrangler enters. The cowgirl is confused at this sudden interest in her person, and the only thing she can think of doing is to give each of the young men a comradely shove. The young men have little time to reflect on the situation, for the rancher's daughter now enters. The wrangler disappears with her; the champion roper, a little peeved at both girls, likewise disappears, and the cowgirl is left alone. Three couples then come in and dance together. When the roper returns, the cowgirl makes a bold decision. She leaps wildly at him, as if she were still on horseback, but her behavior is inappropriate. After a community dance the roper performs a brief exhibitionist solo, and then forgetting that the cowgirl is a girl, nonchalantly rests his arm on her shoulder. Her annoyance increases, but he persuades her to try to dance with him. He does a couple of steps, and she does likewise. But the cowgirl's pleasure is spoiled when the rancher's daughter dances in with the wrangler; abruptly she runs away. Everyone else continues dancing, and the roper consoles himself by dancing along with the others.

The gay dance is interrupted by the cowgirl's reappearance. The dancers are so surprised at the cowgirl's metamorphosis that they can not go on. She has exchanged her riding clothes for a bright red dress (she has kept only her boots), and there are red bows on her braids. The roper does not take long to make up his mind. Taking the attractive cowgirl in his arms, he leads her to the floor, and the dance resumes. The wrangler cuts in. The cowgirl does a solo and shows that she, too, can be feminine. The music stops once more. One of the girls feels unwell and goes out quickly. Then there is a *pas de trois* by the cowgirl, the roper, and the wrangler. The wrangler tries to kiss the cowgirl, but the roper roughly pulls him away; then the roper gives the cowgirl a big kiss to show everybody that he, and not the wrangler, is her man.

The ballet ends with a dance by all the couples.

Rodeo is typically American not only because of the square dances and the riding but even more so because of the theme— "the problem which has never ceased to occupy them [the women] throughout the history of the building of the country: *how to get a suitable man.*" No matter how much one may be averse to the relationships between men and women and between parents and children in America, and especially the dominant role of women, this can not be regarded as a dismal development of our times but as a necessary consequence of previous conditions. America's pioneer men were wild, half vagabond, enterprising, crude, fighting fellows who had to be snared, led, guided, and trained by the equally energetic women. It was not an easy task. It was the women who shaped American society. These women were not the pretty, passionate Spanish girls and women of Mexico (cf. *Billy the Kid*), but the pioneering North American women. That is why the American recognizes *Rodeo* as a thoroughly American work. We can even say that it is the national ballet epic even more than the captivating *Billy the Kid,* which often lays claim to the title because it brings a historical figure on the stage.

At the première the cowgirl was danced by Agnes de Mille; Frederic Franklin was the champion roper; Casimir Kokitch was the head wrangler; and Mlada Miladova was the rancher's daughter. When the ballet was transferred to the repertory of Ballet Theatre (1950) John Kriza succeeded Franklin, and the roper turned out to be one of his most brilliant roles. Agnes de Mille was subsequently replaced by Allyn McLerie, Jenny Workman, Christine Mayer, and Ady Addor.

Cinderella

Ballet in three acts, four scenes. Book: H. D. Volkova, after Perrault's fable. Choreography: Konstantin Sergeyev. Music: Serge Prokofiev. Scenery and costumes: B. R. Erdmann. Première: Spring, 1944, at Molotov, Russia.

CHARACTERS: Cinderella; the prince; Cinderella's father; the stepmother and her two daughters; the good fairy; spring, summer, autumn, and winter fairies; retinues of the four fairies; dancing teacher; master of ceremonies; courtiers; purveyors; court jester; young men; a mazurka couple; foreign guests; three oranges; a Negro boy; courtiers; Spanish and other exotic women; ministers; citizens; grasshoppers and dragonflies; stars; snowflakes; flowers.

ACT I. A room in the house where Cinderella lives. A portrait of Cinderella's deceased mother hangs on a wall. The stepmother and two daughters are busy making a shawl. Cinderella is sitting by the fire.

The stepsisters quarrel about the shawl and thereby anger their mother, who finally takes scissors and cuts the shawl in two. The girls fall to the floor in rage. They soon get up, however, because their only thought is "how to catch a man." Mother and daughters leave the room. Cinderella rises and goes to the portrait of her mother. Her father comes in and sees her standing near the painting. With a reproachful look she shows him the portrait, and he puts a protective arm around the girl. Now his wife comes in and, seeing the two of them standing before the portrait of her predecessor, becomes angry. Suddenly an old woman enters the room and asks for charity. The stepmother refuses her, but Cinderella takes the last piece of bread she has and gives it to the old woman, who thanks her and disappears as mysteriously as she had entered. Now purveyors arrive with ornaments and gloves. The stepsisters fall upon all these pretty things and adorn themselves with them; the stepmother tries to do likewise.

The dancing master comes to give the sisters their last lesson for the gavotte that they must be able to do at the ball; they are very clumsy at it. Cinderella looks on from the hearth. She, too, would like to go to the ball but her stepmother won't permit it.

Preparations for the party continue; the purveyors leave, bowing; and the mother and daughters get ready to go. One of the sisters comes back to stick her tongue out at Cinderella.

Cinderella, left alone, tries the steps of the gavotte; she then thinks of a handsome young man and begins a waltz. The mysterious old woman now reappears, and Cinderella pours out her heart to her. The old woman, who is really a good fairy, promises Cinderella that she will be at the ball and will be the most beautiful of all. Out of her bag she conjures up a pair of lovely slippers. Then the spring fairy dances in with her retinue, bringing a pink and white dress for Cinderella. While the fairy dances, Cinderella is dressed. The summer fairy now enters with her suite. They bring Cinderella roses, the symbol of love. Grasshoppers and dragonflies appear with a stately coach to take Cinderella to the ball. Next comes the autumn fairy with her retinue; they give Cinderella a train in handsome autumn colors. The winter fairy gives her a brilliant ornament and dances with her retinue of snowflakes.

Cinderella is now dressed for the ball. The old woman (the good fairy) tells Cinderella firmly that she must leave the ball before midnight because the spell will be broken at the last stroke of the hour.

All dance as Cinderella climbs into the carriage.

ACT II. A great hall in the palace, with many balustrades, staircases, and a throne.

As the curtain rises, the guests are dancing a pavane. The prince has not yet arrived. The stepmother and her daughters enter the hall. Since it is known that the sisters would bring a big dowry, two partners spring forward to invite them to dance. The four dance, but the dance does not go very well. The master of ceremonies calls for one more mazurka, which is interrupted by the entrance of the prince. The four friends accompanying him do a dance, and then the interrupted mazurka is continued. The master of ceremonies endeavors to get the prince to join the dance, but the prince seems disinclined to do so. A clear bright note is heard at the door, and the prince looks in that direction.

Cinderella stands in the doorway, radiantly beautiful. All bow. She passes through the hall as lightly as a bird and goes up to the prince's throne; he looks at her in delight. A waltz begins. Cinderella dances a solo. The stepmother and stepsisters look on admiringly, not suspecting that it is Cinderella. Cinderella dances another solo, and then there is a solo by the prince. Trays with fruit and beverages are carried around by servants. Cinderella takes the finest fruits there—three oranges, which she presents to her stepmother and stepsisters. A dance by the stepsisters with the three oranges follows. Cinderella dances a *pas de deux* with the prince.

The guests, who had gone off to take a brief rest, return at the sound of a merry waltz. The gaiety is at its height, and Cinderella entirely forgets the old fairy's warning. Dwarfs come over to remind her of the midnight hour and, just before the last stroke sounds, Cinderella runs out. On the steps she discovers she is once more wearing her old gray dress. In her haste to get away before anyone sees her, she loses one of her pretty little slippers. The prince who has noticed Cinderella's departure, hurries after her, but finds only the slipper on the steps. He picks it up and presses it to his heart.

ACT III, SCENE 1. The prince has ordered all the shoemakers to appear before him. He wants to know who made the slipper and who its owner is, but none of the shoemakers recognizes the little slipper. The prince, determined not to rest until he has found the girl whose foot fits the slipper, decides to go on a journey.

Preparations are made, and the prince departs. The first girl he meets is a Russian, but when, after her galop, she tries to put the slipper on, she finds that her foot is too big. The journey continues. Two Spanish girls try the slipper on, but it does not fit them either. The prince travels further but at last returns home unsuccessful.

ACT III, SCENE 2. The room in Cinderella's house. Cinderella is asleep in a corner. When she awakes, she reminisces about the splendid ball. She takes the slipper from her blouse and looks at it wistfully; she picks up a broom and dances with it as if the broom were her beloved prince.

As footsteps are heard, Cinderella quickly hides the slipper. The stepsisters come in with their oranges and tell Cinderella of their success at the ball. Another quarrel begins and once more the stepsisters end up squabbling on the floor, as Cinderella looks on smiling. Women and girls enter with news: The prince is looking in every house for the girl that lost a slipper on the steps of his palace.

The prince arrives amid great confusion. The two stepsisters stick out their big clumsy feet. Even the stepmother wants to try the slipper on and orders Cinderella to help her. Cinderella kneels down, and, as she does so, the matching slipper falls out of her blouse. The prince looks at it with amazement. Then he takes Cinderella by the arm to help her up and recognizes her as the belle of his ball. The good fairy enters again and changes the room into a fairy garden. The lovers will never more be parted.

◈

In the Russian première Galina Ulanova danced the title role, with Mikhail Gabovich as her partner. In 1945, Rostislav Zakharov revised the ballet for the Bolshoi Theater.

Frederick Ashton has also created a *Cinderella* to Prokofiev's music. The première of this full-length ballet (the first all-English three-act classical ballet) was presented on December 23, 1948, at Covent Garden, London, by the Sadler's Wells Ballet. Moira Shearer danced the title role; Michael Somes was the prince; and Robert Helpmann and Frederick Ashton played the stepsisters.

There are several differences between the English and Russian versions. For example, Ashton has men perform the roles of the stepsisters, and the pantomime interpretation indicates that they are old maids. Ballerinas portray the stepsisters in the Russian version and rightly so because ugly old maids would no longer expect to marry; therefore they wouldn't be interested in attending the prince's ball or in forcing the slipper to fit their foot. Furthermore, in the Russian version the personalities of the sisters are different—one is good, the other bad. In the English version a portrait of Cinderella's own mother hangs in Act I and Act III; in the Russian version pictures of both Cinderella's real mother and her stepmother are hanging, the former covered by a curtain which Cinderella later removes. The Russians have Cinderella hurrying down the steps with the prince after her; the English have her pressing through the crowded guests to a gate through which she escapes. The British version also omits the prince's search for his beloved through foreign lands and depicts the lovers at the end departing for home in a boat, as fairy-tale characters wave farewell.

Two other choreographers have created *Cinderella* to Prokofiev's music—Victor Gsovsky and Daisy Spies. Gsovsky's work was first performed at the Bavarian Opera in Munich in 1951 with Irène Skorik in the title role, Heino Hallhuber as the prince, and Sill Spindler and Walther Matthes as the stepsisters. The Spies ballet was first performed at the Berlin Staatsoper in 1951.

In the history of ballet a number of other works have been based on the Perrault story. Charles Didelot is said to have designed a *Cendrillon*. And another Frenchman, Albert (François Decombe), presented *Cendrillon* at the Paris Opéra on March 3, 1823. This ballet was produced the following year in Moscow by Feliciata Hullin-Sor, the *maîtresse de ballet*. In 1906 Adeline Genée appeared in London as Cinderella in a work choreographed by Fred Farren. And Michel Fokine mounted a *Cendrillon* for the 1939 Covent Garden Educational Ballet Season.

The best-known early *Cinderella,* however, was that of Marius Petipa, whose work, in collaboration with Enrico Cecchetti and Lev Ivanov, was first presented in 1893. The book was by Lydia Pashkova, scenery and costumes by G. Levogt, M. Shiskov, and M. Botcharov, and music by B. Schell. The cast included the prince's father and mother and a cook and her helpers (who opened the ballet with a dance in the kitchen with kitchen utensils) but omitted the fairies of the seasons and the good fairy who was responsible for Cinderella's metamorphosis. When Cinderella is recognized as the owner of the slipper, the stepsisters beg her forgiveness. Principals at the première were Pierina Legnani (Cinderella), Paul Gerdt (Prince), Mathilde Kchesinska and M. K. Andersen (stepsisters).

This fairy-tale ballet is suitable for large companies able to meet the expense of an elaborate production.

Fancy Free

Comic ballet in one act. Book and choreography: Jerome Robbins. Music: Leonard Bernstein. Scenery: Oliver Smith. Costumes: Kermit Love. Première: April 18, 1944, at the Metropolitan Opera House, New York, by Ballet Theatre.

CHARACTERS: three sailors, a brunette; a redhead; a blonde; a barkeeper.

❧

The curtain rises on a quiet stage. It is a hot summer evening in New York. On the left is the interior of a bar, whose entrance is in the center of the stage. On the right, outside the bar, is the street corner with a big, slanting, lighted lamppost and a sidewalk.

A sailor comes tumbling in, stopping at the bar entrance. The music begins, and two more sailors land in front of the bar in the same way. The three men are obviously out for a good time—that is, looking for pretty girls. Anything that looks like fun is welcome. These three madcaps seem to be good friends. After spinning about a bit, they stand side by side. What shall they do? They stand hopefully, but when nothing happens, they decide to go into the bar for a drink. The barkeeper gives them beer, and the sailors gulp it down. Who is to pay? They decide to choose by the number of fingers they put out. But one connives with the second, and the third is the victim. Obviously he is used to this because he shakes his head and pays as if he had expected to be the loser. Then they straighten their uniforms a little and go outside refreshed.

Again, they wait for something to happen. The friends take sticks of gum and toss the wrappers into the air. A brunette enters from the left. She comes up to the sailors with catlike movements. The three sailors stand there watching her. Their heads move like one as they follow her movements. The sailors are carried along by the rhythm of the dance. They take her handbag. The girl pretends to be angry, but she knows it is only a joke. The bag travels from one to another. The girl stamps her foot. Finally she gets her bag back and leaves, followed by two of the sailors. The sailor who is left alone is in luck. A still more attractive young lady, a redhead, comes along. As if by accident he stumbles into her so that he can get acquainted. He lifts her up and invites her to have a drink in the bar. The lights go out.

The couple is now sitting at the bar. The sailor drinks a beer; the redhead makes a show of leaving. But fearing to lose his newly found acquaintance too soon, the sailor invites her to dance. The most interesting *pas de deux* in the ballet follows: It is the encounter of two young people who find each other attractive. The girl dances in high heels, not in ballet slippers. Finally the sailor pays the check, gives the girl his arm, and is about to leave with her when his two friends come back with their girl. Everyone is introduced, and they all go back to the bar. They order drinks and sit down at the table; the barkeeper brings the beer. The girls, who turn out to know each other, go off to the side and chat gaily. The young men are occupied with the problem of two girls to three boys, and they prepare for a little friendly competition. The girls return to the boys at the table. Now one of the sailors gets up and begins a solo. This solo exhibits the sailor in all his crudeness and lack of conventional forms of politeness. The girls look on and incite him to show them his tricks. It is not so much a matter of impressing the girls as of showing himself off. When the sailor has danced himself out, the friends are ready to leave; but now the girls hold them back. The second sailor begins his solo by a glide over the floor and leaps over the bar stools; finally he falls down in pretended adoration at the feet of the girls. Now it is the turn of the last sailor to show his tricks. His dance is more gliding and flowing, more directly ingratiating. The girls and boys dance a Lindy Hop together, during which the boys finally lose control of themselves and get into a fight. The girls are a little frightened, for the boys seem to have gone crazy. They jump in back of the bar and continue their battle there, or at least we see arms and legs projecting from the bar. The barkeeper stays calm through all this and takes the opportunity to clear the glasses off the table. The girls decide they had better make their getaway. The young men are so busy fighting that they do not notice the girls' departure and are disconcerted; when they have finally had enough of the battle, they find that the girls are gone. They straighten their clothes and run out to see whether the girls are anywhere to be found. No one is in sight. They look at their scratches and at their dirty clothes; then the humor of the situation dawns on them, and they begin to laugh. They slap each other on the shoulder and are highly pleased with their adventure. That calls for another drink.

They return to the bar for another beer and once more play the game about paying—with the same result as before. Then they go outside and look around, leaning on each other like true comrades. The evening is young yet. A new adventure is still a possibility. A pretty blonde comes from the left. She dances a solo. The sailors are once more enchanted by feminine beauty. Their entire bodies follow the movements of the blonde, who goes off. Should they follow her? Yes or no? Should they try another adventure? Better not, better let her go. But one of them weakens and goes after her; the others follow.

❧

Jerome Robbins created this work during the Second World War, when America was developing a great interest in the art of dance; full purses were available and people needed something to take their minds off the war. There is nothing especially "navy" about Robbins' three sailors; they are typical youths looking for girls and trying to enliven their situation. In a certain sense, *Fancy Free* becomes a timeless ballet, for the problem of youths seeking social contacts is always similar—whether in Ovid's time, today, or tomorrow. Bernstein's music is workmanlike. The scenery and costumes are appropriate for the theme of the ballet and contribute to the atmosphere. The original cast was comprised of John Kriza, Harold Lang, Jerome Robbins, Muriel Bentley, Janet Reed, and Shirley Eckl.

Les Forains ("Showmen at the Fair")

Ballet in one act. Book: Boris Kochno. Choreography: Roland Petit. Music: Henri Sauguet. Scenery and costumes: Christian Bérard. Première: March 2, 1945, at the Théâtre des Champs-Elysées, Paris, by the Ballets des Champs-Elysées.

CHARACTERS: conjurer (also the leader); clown; female acrobat; shadow players; Siamese twins; dream apparition; Sleeping Beauty; audience.

❧

The curtain rises on an empty stage. A girl, dressed in a skirt and blouse, comes in from the left and does a dance on her toes, waving a small fan. Then a handcart drawn by two figures appears from the left. It is loaded with poles and canvas; on top of it sits a girl holding a cage with pigeons. They are showmen; one of the men (the clown of the company) still has some white on his face. Now the leader of the wretched troupe arrives. One of the acrobats supports a little girl on his arm; the girl is obviously very tired. The leader decides that the tents should be erected again. The players are hungry, and their last receipts were slim. The cart is emptied, and the tent put up. Those not engaged in erecting the tent sit down listlessly. Two of the girls take off their coats and start to rehearse. Then the clown and the acrobat perform the beginning of their number. The tent is now almost ready. The leader gives the signal for rehearsal. He shakes the tired players and rouses them for the general opening. One acrobat performs handstands, and another spins around rapidly. Spectators gather. The artists go into the tent; the performance is about to begin. The lights go out; the stage remains entirely dark. The lights go on, and some shadows on the tent canvas can be seen. Then the canvas parts, and the clown and the young girl acrobat come forward. A simple chair is placed in the center of the stage. The clown tries to get the attention of the audience by high leaps. The acrobat shows the young girl some tricks. After the two exit, a dancer appears with a great white veil. She is called a "vision d'art," an apparition, and does a veil dance. The many-colored lights thrown by the projectors suggest a figure from *The Arabian Nights*. After her solo she disappears into the tent.

The clown enters again. He astonishes the audience with great leaps and turns. Then the Siamese twins appear. Two girls, tied together by a dress, execute a dance in which they express their link and their fate. It is a very simple dance on *pointes*.

The conjurer now comes out of the tent with a leap, throws streamers into the air, scatters confetti, and finally produces from a canvas bag a bouquet of flowers which he offers to a spectator. Then comes the big stunt: He conjures a chest, from which rises Sleeping Beauty. The dance she executes is that of a mechanical doll. A *pas de deux* with the conjurer is ended by the sudden upward flight of a pair of pigeons, which are caught by the other members of the company. All the players now reassemble to show their skills once more in the finale. The audience applauds; the leader wants to solicit their appreciation in material terms, but the spectators leave. The players are left empty-handed.

The German occupation of Paris completely stifled ballet art at the Opéra. During the war there had been only sporadic attempts at reviving the ballet there, and once the city was liberated, Lifar, who was regarded as a collaborator of the enemy, was temporarily removed from his post.

Nevertheless, even during the war years, French ballet art did experience a revival—given impetus by the work of Boris Kochno (who had once been associated with Diaghilev), Irène Lidova, and the young impresario Claude Giraud. New choreographies were produced on "Friday evenings" without restriction, and composers and designers began to donate their services. Two young choreographer-dancers who were watched with greatest interest and hope were Janine Charrat and Roland Petit. *Les Forains*, Petit's first major ballet, made him world famous. Its success was so great that within a few years after its first presentation it had been performed five hundred times.

Les Forains is a dramatic ballet with acrobatic inserts based on standard ballet technique. There is little structure; the beginning and the end are set to the same musical theme; and in between the "form" flows out of the content. At the première Roland Petit, Janine Charrat, and Ethery Pagava danced the principal roles.

Interplay

Ballet in four movements. Choreography: Jerome Robbins. Music: Morton Gould. Scenery: Oliver Smith. Costumes: Irene Sharaff. Première: June 1, 1945, at the Ziegfeld Theatre, New York, in Billy Rose's Concert Varieties.

CHARACTERS: four boys and four girls.

Interplay is partially based on American children's games; the dances present a constant interplay between classical dance steps and contemporary rhythms. It has no literary subject, no story or drama; it is thus what is called an abstract ballet. The structure is not complicated. Robbins chose for his patterns (which do not go beyond the basic dances of the Baroque) the diagonal, the

front line, the circle, and the serpentine. The eye is attracted especially by quick changes of the pattern and a certain youthful un-
concern. For example, we find the basic patterns at the beginning
of the ensemble and never thereafter. The jazz-like music to which
the ensemble is danced is replaced by romantic music for the *pas
de deux.*

At the Ziegfeld Theatre the principal roles were danced by
John Kriza, Janet Reed, and Jerome Robbins. Harold Lang re-
placed Robbins when the work was taken into the repertory of
Ballet Theatre on October 17, 1945, with new décor by Oliver
Smith and Irene Sharaff. The New York City Ballet added
Interplay to its repertory on December 23, 1952.

Night Shadow ("La Sonnambula")

*Ballet in one act. Book: Vittorio Rieti. Choreography: George
Balanchine. Music: Vincenzo Bellini, arranged by Vittorio Rieti.
Scenery and costumes: Dorothea Tanning. Première: February 27,
1946, at the New York City Center, by the Ballet Russe de Monte
Carlo.*

CHARACTERS: a baron (also the host); his wife (also the sleepwalker); a coquette; a poet; guests; Negroes; acrobats; harlequin.

The ballet takes place about 1840 in a great castle. The baron,
with the coquette at his side, is greeting the guests. Then all
participate in the usual social dances of the time; masked, they
dance in pairs, in lines and rings, or in small groups. A little later
the poet enters. The baron greets him coldly and introduces him
to the coquette. The poet politely kisses her hand. The baron announces a *divertissement.* First, two girls in Watteau-like costumes
dance a kind of pastoral, then a Negro man and woman do a
comical *pas de deux,* and finally three acrobats come in with hoops,
with which they dance a *pas de trois.*

The dance music sounds again. The couples take off their masks
and go into the garden. The poet and the coquette remain behind

and dance together. When the other guests return, they decide to play blindman's buff and the poet succeeds in catching the coquette. Then the couples form a chain with their arms upraised and leave the hall, the baron taking the coquette with him. The poet is left alone.

Night falls. A light appears in front of one of the castle windows. In a little while a silent apparition in nightdress enters the room with a candlestick in her hand. It is the baron's wife, walking in her sleep. The poet, enraptured, tries to awaken her. He dances around her, lies down before her, and even touches her. Finally the temptation is too strong for him, and when she leaves, he follows her. Just then the coquette comes on stage for a quick meeting with the poet. Jealous, she tells the baron what she has just seen. The baron feels that he has been injured, draws his sword, and leaves to find the poet. As the guests come on stage again, the poet stumbles in with a hand to his side. He falls dead before them. The sleepwalker glides expressionless across the stage. The guests take the poet on their shoulders to carry him out, but the sleepwalker takes the poet from them and carries him in her arms off to her room.

The ballet is based on a dramatic subject, but the principal impression is derived from the poet's efforts to arouse or establish a rapport with the sleepwalker. He puts his arms around her, but she escapes without apparently seeing him; he lies down in front of her, and she steps over him; he changes her direction, and she goes further (still on *pointes*), sometimes in rapid tempo. Is it his dream? Yes, but it will be his death. And it is only when he is dead that the sleepwalker recognizes him and carries him off in her arms like a mother. This is a symbolic ballet, and here, too, Balanchine is a great master. Jean Aumer mounted a ballet with the same name for the Paris Opéra on September 19, 1827, but the two works have nothing in common, not even the music.

At the première Alexandra Danilova was the sleepwalker; Nicholas Magallanes, the poet; Maria Tallchief, the coquette; and Michel Katcharoff, the host. John Taras rehearsed the work with members of the Marquis de Cuevas Ballet, where Maria

Tallchief and Ethery Pagava alternated as the sleepwalker and George Skibine appeared as the poet. The work is also in the repertory of the New York City Ballet, the Royal Danish Ballet, and Sonia Gaskell's Netherlands Ballet. *Étude* was its name at its première in Denmark, where it was danced by Margot Lander, Hans Brenaa, and Svend Eric Jensen. The ballet is very popular in Europe.

The figure of Harlequin, omitted in some performances, was restored in the New York City Ballet revival for Edward Villela.

Symphony in C ("Palais de Cristal")

Ballet in four parts. Choreography: George Balanchine. Music: Georges Bizet. Scenery and costumes: Léonor Fini. Première: July 28, 1947, at the Opéra, Paris.

PART I: Allegro vivo.

The first part is danced by a small *corps de ballet* of six girls and by three couples. Each couple does its own dances. We can not speak here of a *pas de deux* proper, since the soloists virtually form a unit with the *corps de ballet*. At the end, a short *pas de trois* and some solos are introduced.

PART II: Adagio.

The choreographer takes advantage of the opportunity to develop his favorite play of lines. There are many square formations, after which there are diagonals. The *corps de ballet* is in almost constant motion in place, in order to support the solo work. Balanchine does not hold the dancers of the *corps* so strictly in place as was the custom with the choreographers of the romantic ballet; they move quietly over short distances.

PART III: Allegro vivace.

A *pas de deux* in a rectilinear setting, finally crossed by a diagonal.

PART IV: Allegro vivace.

Here Balanchine draws splendid lines in space. In the finale the groups of the first three parts unite, the entire ensemble moving in the usual manner from front to rear, from left to right, and diagonally across the stage.

In 1947 George Balanchine was invited to the Paris Opéra to stage revivals of several of his ballets. When he finished, he wished to create a new work for the principal dancers of the Opéra. He chose, as seemed appropriate, music by a French composer: the recently discovered *Bizet Symphony,* which Bizet had composed at the age of seventeen for a Prix de Rome competition. Each movement had a different dance scheme and development and its own ballerina, *danseur,* and *corps de ballet*—with all principals, soloists, and *corps* appearing on stage together for a brilliant finale. The cast for the first performance included Lycette Darsonval, Tamara Toumanova, Micheline Bardin, Madeleine Lafon, Alexandre Kalioujny, Roger Ritz, Michel Renault, and Max Bozzoni. On March 22, 1948, it was first presented in the United States by the Ballet Society (later the New York City Ballet) with Maria Tallchief, Tanaquil LeClercq, Beatrice Tompkins, Elise Reiman, Nicholas Magallanes, Francisco Moncion, Herbert Bliss, and Lew Christensen in the principal roles. There was no scenery—only a blue cyclorama—and all the costumes were white (in sharp contrast to the berry tints of the Paris production). *Symphony in C* has also been staged for the Royal Danish Ballet (première, October 4, 1952).

Études ("Étude")

Ballet in one act. Choreography: Harald Lander. Music: Études *by Czerny, arranged by the Danish composer Knudage Riisager. Scenery: Norgreen. Première: January 15, 1948, at the Royal Theater, Copenhagen, by the Royal Danish Ballet, under the name* Étude.

The ballet contains eighteen parts and represents nothing more than the development of the ballet dancer. We thus see various phases of ballet training and the demands made on the pupil.

In the beginning twelve girls in black tutus are practicing at the bar. The more difficult exercises are executed by girls in white tutus and boys in light gray *maillots*. Then comes the work "au milieu" (in the center, away from the bar), rehearsing a *pas de trois*, a *pas de deux*, a *pas de quatre*, a *pas de six*, and *corps de ballet* work. The high point comes with the technical stunts of the soloists. A finale with all the collaborators concludes the ballet.

Lander's work is pure ballet, based entirely on classic technique, and it evidences Lander's excellent work in the Danish school. *Études* lasts half an hour, and the spectator watches it with growing tension and delight. After Lander left the Danish Ballet, he rehearsed *Études* with dancers of the Paris Opéra, where it had its première on November 19, 1952. He also mounted it in London for Anton Dolin's Festival Ballet (première, August 8, 1955) with his wife Toni Lander, John Gilpin, Polajenko, and Dolin in the principal roles, and for the American Ballet Theatre (première, October 15, 1961) with Toni Lander, Royes Fernandez, and Bruce Martos in the leading roles.

Carmen

Ballet in five scenes. Book: taken from Meilhac and Halévy's "opéra comique." Choreography: Roland Petit. Music: Georges Bizet. Scenery and costumes: Antoni Clavé. Première: February 21, 1949, at the Prince's Theatre, London, by Roland Petit's Ballets de Paris.

CHARACTERS: Carmen; Don José; toreador; bandits; cigarette makers.

SCENE 1. Marching music is heard. The curtain rises on a dark stage which gradually becomes light, revealing a street in Seville. In the center rear is the gray wall of a cigarette factory, and on the left, a flight of stairs leading to the factory. Lines of wash hang across the street.

Some men, sitting against the wall of the factory, are playing cards; they are unattractive in appearance. Several factory girls come down the stairs and join the men in a dance that is quickly broken up by the noise of a fight between two girls, one of whom is Carmen. As the girls descend the stairs Carmen seems about ready to strangle the other girl. The soldier Don José separates the girls and arrests Carmen, who begins to use her feminine charms to win her freedom. She smiles ingratiatingly and suddenly vanishes. Don José is bewitched by her beauty.

SCENE 2. Night. A tavern. To the left, a large oil lamp; to the right, a bright-colored Japanese lantern, which throws a shimmering light. In the background are a number of grayish-white arches, and a staircase on the left leads to rooms above. A red curtain covers the door.

Men and women in the room are talking, standing, just sitting, or flirting. Four couples dance to castanets.

Don José enters and looks around in wonder. The men are a little surprised at his coming but shrug their shoulders. They pick up the chairs, put them in a row near the arches, and invite Don José to dance. He consents and does a habañera.

Carmen, who has been observing unseen from a corner, comes up to Don José and dances a few seductive steps, using her fan. Two bandits lift her up; then Carmen continues her solo, faster and faster, to the rhythm of the clapping. At the end she falls on one knee before Don José. As he looks at her breathless, the red-headed bandit steals his watch chain; another one takes his watch. But nothing except Carmen exists for Don José: He takes her in his arms and carries her upstairs.

Inspired by Carmen's conquest, one of the girls dances with two of the bandits (*pas de trois*). Then all the customers join in the feverish merrymaking.

Carmen and Don José appear at the head of the stairs, then slowly descend. To the rhythm of handclapping and the stamping of feet, the lovers dance faster and faster. Suddenly Don José stops the dance, takes his cape off, and places it around Carmen's shoulders; the two leave together.

SCENE 3. The curtain rises on a yellow drop curtain, which Don José pushes aside to reveal Carmen's shabby room. On the right is an old wash basin and a jug on a table. A curtain hangs on one side. In the middle of the room is a white iron bed with a faded spread. Left of center, a window opens out on a street, and in the distance a sunlit mountain landscape spreads out. Some fans on the wall are the only decoration.

Carmen wearing a black corset trimmed in blue is sitting on the bed biting her nails. Don José has washed and dried his hands and goes over to her. When he sits down Carmen gets up and begins a languid dance; she lingers at the window and looks out. Don José, suspecting that she is looking at a rival, immediately goes over to her. She keeps on dancing and moves as if to leave the room. But Don José holds her back, and there follows a very erotic *pas de deux,* the famous, magnificent bedroom scene. At the moment that Carmen puts her cheek tenderly against Don José's, the bandits come in to get Carmen. She changes her tone and scolds Don José, telling him he would be better off doing his duty; but Don José is bewitched by Carmen and follows the unsavory troupe.

Scene 4. A deserted carriage shed, surrounded by a fence. The weak light of two lanterns shows old wheels hanging under a grayish-green canvas stretched on some poles.

The redheaded bandit, Carmen, her friends, and Don José come up on their tiptoes and plan to rob a man who will be coming by soon with money. Don José, designated to give the fatal blow, is handed a dagger. He is opposed to killing someone that he is not interested in merely to steal money; but, they tell him, the only way he can get Carmen's love is thus to compromise himself. The bandits hide, and Don José practices with the dirk. At the sound of approaching footsteps he retreats into the shadows, then jumps out at his victim, and stabs him in the heart. Carmen looks on from behind one of the wagon wheels. The man falls, and the sound of jingling gold is heard. The bandits come out of their hiding place, take the booty, and run off. Don José is left alone with his victim.

Scene 5. The entrance to a bull ring. Above a red fence are the faces of the audience.

Some gypsies are performing; they are being watched by a group of girls, including Carmen. Attention is suddenly diverted by the coming of the toreador, a self-satisfied man who enjoys answering the greetings of the girls. He boasts of his forthcoming victory over the bull in the arena. Carmen is greatly impressed by the toreador and wants to follow him inside. Don José, who has been hiding nearby, now springs out and stops her, as the others enter the arena. Carmen and Don José are alone. They measure their strength for a moment. Then Don José leaps at Carmen and tears off her mantilla. A long *pas de deux* follows, in which Carmen rejects Don José. They glare at each other, and Carmen instinctively feels the danger hanging over her. Don José will not let her go. He takes the dagger; Carmen throws herself at him, and Don José strikes. Slowly Carmen sinks lifeless to the ground, while Don José stands astride her body. Then the victory march of the toreador is heard. The spectators throw their hats up in the air in enthusiasm.

Roland Petit was a sudden star in the Paris firmament. As a choreographer he is uneven in his accomplishments, but he has the gift of a great feeling for theater. A year before he created *Carmen,* he was invited by the man who was his impresario at that time to see a performance of the opera *Carmen.* Petit was bored in his loge seat and in a little while said he did not want to see any more of the performance; the two men left the theater. Then twelve months later Petit suggested the idea of a *Carmen* ballet. He pieced together various parts of Bizet's music, helter-skelter, to the great indignation of many music and opera lovers. For example, he himself danced Carmen's habañera. But the result was a work of theater such as we seldom see. Instead of Spanish dance steps, he used steps from the ballet vocabulary. Here and there he used castanets. The settings by the Spaniard Clavé are simple, refined, and attractive.

Renée Jeanmaire danced the role of Carmen; Roland Petit, the part of Don José; Gordon Hamilton and Teddy Rodolphe, the two bandits; Jane Laoust, the bandit girl; and Serge Perrault, the toreador. During the years that *Carmen* was performed by the Ballets de Paris, circumstances dictated changes in casting.

Miss Julie

Ballet in four scenes. Book: after the play of the same name by August Strindberg. Choreography: Birgit Cullberg. Music: Ture

Rangström, orchestrated by Hans Grossman. Scenery and costumes: Allan Fridericia. Première: March 1, 1950, at Västerås, Sweden, in a performance organized by Riksteatern.

CHARACTERS: Miss Julie; her father, the count; her fiancé; Jean, the servant; Kristin, the cook; Clara; Ebba; Svea; inhabitants of the region.

SCENE 1. The ballroom in a castle. A summer evening around 1880. The curtain rises on a drop curtain depicting a castle. After a few moments the curtain parts, revealing the ballroom of the castle. Portraits of ancestors are on the walls.

A group of young girls enters with garlands, which they use to decorate the family portraits. The midsummer night festival is to be held that evening. While the girls are working, Jean comes into the room. The girls play tricks on him, but Jean is evidently used to that. Jean takes advantage of the festive mood to steal a kiss from Clara, the forester's daughter. At this moment Miss Julie appears in the doorway and looks ironically at Jean and Clara. Then she discovers the decorations on the paintings. She is not at all an admirer of her ancestors' faces and directs the girls to remove the garlands. After they have complied, they leave the room, taking the garlands with them. Julie is now alone with Jean.

Julie has just returned from her ride. She stalks past Jean, smiling mysteriously, and gives him a gentle tap on the cheek with her riding crop.

Then the count enters with the fiancé he has chosen for his daughter. Jean stands back humbly. The count puts his daughter's hand in the hand of the fiancé and goes off, happy and contented. Julie is not so well pleased with her father's choice and works out a plan to get rid of the fiancé. As if in jest she invites him to jump over the riding crop which she holds up. He accepts the challenge and repeats the leap over and over again until he sees the sarcastic smile of his betrothed. He flies into a rage and in the ensuing dispute throws Julie to the floor, tosses his ring away, and leaves the hall. Julie sits on the floor, shakes her head, shrugs her shoulders, and tosses her ring away, too. Then she gets up and goes to the door to look at the merrymakers.

SCENE 2. The barn of the castle. A weak light comes from the lanterns hanging on the beams. At the right is a beer barrel on which are a number of glasses.

The merrymakers are dancing; Jean is with Clara. Suddenly Julie appears in the doorway. Everyone is surprised to see the count's daughter among them. She is wearing a very décolleté summer dress. After a brief hesitation she enters the barn, goes over to Jean, and asks him to dance with her. The amazement increases. Jean hesitates for a moment, then takes his master's daughter in his arms, and leads her in the dance, which becomes wilder and wilder. It can be seen that everyone is asking himself whether this is proper behavior for the count's daughter. Suddenly Jean leaves Julie and goes out of the barn; Julie is left standing alone on the dance floor. One of the men, who has drunk more than is good for him, thinks that he can do as he pleases and offers to take her in his arms. Julie pushes him off angrily and runs out of the barn.

SCENE 3. The kitchen. On the left is a door that leads to Jean's room.

Kristin the cook is stirring something in a bowl. Jean comes in and tells her what has just happened in the barn. Then he begins to flirt with Kristin. Julie enters and looks on. It is late. Kristin takes her apron off, gets ready to go to bed, and leaves the kitchen.

Julie is now alone with Jean again. She provokes her father's servant so far that he kisses her hand and even her feet. Julie, relaxed, leans against the kitchen table and stretches like a kitten. Jean has the greatest difficulty controlling himself; the only thing he can think of doing is to polish his master's boots. But Julie again comes to him, tempting him. Jean would like to yield to her advances, but he is afraid of losing his comfortable job. Finally he can withstand her no longer; he takes Julie in his arms, tears off her dress, and kisses her violently.

They are interrupted by the sound of voices and footsteps. Julie realizes that she can not be found by the merrymakers in her slip. She looks around for a place to hide. Jean shows her the door of his room—if she closes the door, no one will find her. After a brief moment of hesitation, Julie enters the room; Jean follows and closes the door behind them.

The merrymakers come in. One of the girls discovers Julie's dress, which is passed from hand to hand, with suitable comments.

Then they go over to Jean's door, which is locked, and they all leave the kitchen frustrated.

Day breaks. Julie comes out of Jean's room with her hair and clothes in disorder. It was obviously not as safe inside as Jean had represented. Jean comes out shortly afterwards with cheerful steps, lies down on the table, and orders Julie to come over to him; he is the boss now. Interrupted by his master's bell, calling for his boots for the morning ride, Jean jumps down. Kristin enters in her Sunday clothes with her Bible under her arm and looks at the pair. Julie goes off in a huff.

Scene 4. The ballroom.

Convinced that she can never face her father again and determined to run off with Jean, Julie comes into the ballroom to take some jewels from the chest to finance her flight. The family portraits look down at her reproachfully. The faces are deformed in her imagination. They surround Julie and lift her up. The leader hands Julie a dagger, with which she can take her life and spare the family a great disgrace. Julie sinks down unconscious.

The sun mounts slowly and sends its rays into the hall. Julie sways, looks around in amazement, and then discovers the dagger in her hand. She puts the point against her breast.

Jean comes in to see whether everything is in order in the hall. Noticing that the jewel chest has fallen to the ground, he goes over to it and puts it back in its place. Then he sees Julie with the dagger in her hand and tries to take it from her. But Julie presses his hand on hers, and the dagger pierces her body. Julie falls. Jean opens the door and walks out.

There is some difference of opinion as to the origin of the subject. Allan Fridericia (the Danish designer, critic, and husband of Else-Marianne von Rosen) asserts that he thought that Strindberg's subject was very well suited for his wife and that he therefore proposed it to Birgit Cullberg.

The Swedish critic Sven Haeger says, however, that he had long previously proposed the matter to Birgit Cullberg in 1949 and that he had suggested *Fröken Julie* or a poem by Froding. After Birgit Cullberg had seen Petit's *Carmen* in the summer of

1950, she decided to rehearse the work. Her friend Hans Grossman looked for a suitable composition for her. Miss Cullberg sketched the work out and danced it for Haeger himself. Thereafter it was decided to prepare the work for Else-Marianne von Rosen and Julius Mengarelli.

The choreographer in an interview in *Dance News*, October, 1958, says that she had long looked for a good interpreter for the role of Miss Julie. Then in 1949 Else-Marianne von Rosen came into Miss Cullberg's small group. After working with von Rosen for a short time, Cullberg became convinced that this ballerina, herself the daughter of a count, would be the right interpreter; in any case the world première was danced by Else-Marianne von Rosen and Mengarelli. Although other ballerinas have appeared as Miss Julie, the general opinion is still that Else-Marianne von Rosen has been the most ideal interpreter of a part that requires excellent classical technique and special ability in pantomime.

The success of the work was so great that the management of the Royal Ballet Theater in Stockholm asked permission to take the ballet into its repertory; the première took place in Stockholm on September 7, 1950, with the part of Miss Julie danced by Gun Skooberg.

The work was first performed in London on February 19, 1951, by the Royal Swedish Ballet with Else-Marianne von Rosen and Mengarelli in the title roles.

The American Ballet Theatre also took the work into its repertory, and Birgit Cullberg went to New York to direct the rehearsals. The New York première was given on September 18, 1958, at the Metropolitan Opera House and was the success of the early season, with Violette Verdy and Erik Bruhn in the principal roles.

The Cage

Ballet in one act. Book and choreography: Jerome Robbins. Music: Igor Stravinsky's "Concerto in D for String Orchestra."

Costumes: Ruth Sobotka. Première: June 14, 1951, at the New York City Center, by the New York City Ballet.

CHARACTERS: the novice; the queen; two intruders; twelve female beings.

❧

Under the dimly lit tangles of a spider-like web are a number of female beings, clothed in tight sand-colored leotards, trimmed with thick, dark cords. In the foreground, left, sits a figure enveloped in a veil. The queen goes up to this figure and unveils her. The new-born stretches her limbs; finally she can stand on her own legs. The newcomer has made her entry into society; the queen and female beings leave her alone.

A young man appears. He tries to catch the novice. In a short struggle she overpowers him, throws him to the ground, and stamps in rage on his face and chest. Then she puts his head between her thighs and breaks his neck. When the young man succumbs, the novice carelessly rolls him aside. The queen and the female beings return to congratulate her.

A second young man enters, and all but he and the novice leave the stage. This young man seems destined for a better fate; for a moment we get the impression that the novice has lost her lust for destruction. She yields to the act of procreation, but as soon as it is completed, the others return. Full of aggression, they rush at the young man, who vainly tries to escape their fury. The novice returns to the attack. Making a gesture with her arms like an insect using its sting, she kills the second intruder as well. All join in a triumphant dance.

❧

This work by Robbins is far from engaging, but it has a powerful effect. It carries conviction by its firmness and brevity and by the shrillness and frankness with which the choreographer operated.

The ballet consists of two long *pas de deux*, set in acrobatic forms and framed by a small *corps de ballet* of twelve dancers and the queen. The novice is the most important soloist. The remarkable thing about the choreography of the *corps de ballet* (in a setting reminiscent of a revue) is that Robbins made only trifling changes in the movements of the pretty chorus girls to transform them into cruel beings. The program notes say: "The choreographer drew his inspiration from definite phenomena in the insect and animal world, as well as from our mythology, in which the female regards the male as her prey. . . . The subject comprises the initiation rites of a mythical cult." But it seems more probable that Robbins was inspired by the position of authority of the American woman.

The principals at the première were Nora Kaye (novice), Yvonne Mounsey (queen), Nicholas Magallanes and Roy Tobias (intruders). Subsequently Tanaquil LeClercq, Melissa Hayden, and Allegra Kent have interpreted the novice and have been effective in their own way. When Jerome Robbins formed his Ballets: U.S.A., he included *The Cage* in the repertory of that company.

Sylvia (II)

Ballet in three acts. Subject: Jules Barbier and Baron de Reinach. Choreography: Frederick Ashton. Music: Léo Delibes. Scenery and Costumes: Robin and Christopher Ironside. Première: September 3, 1952, at Covent Garden, London, by the Sadler's Wells Ballet.

CHARACTERS: Sylvia; Amyntas; Orion; Eros; Orion's slaves; Orion's concubines; Diana; a goat couple; Apollo; the Muses: dance, tragedy, comedy, history, epic poetry, lyric poetry, erotic poetry, astronomy, hymns of praise; Ceres; Jason; Persephone; Pluto; sylphs; nymphs; dryads; naiads; Diana's cortege; villagers; trumpeters.

❧

Basically this is the same ballet as Mérante's (page 50), but there are certain changes that require mention. The first act is danced in a clearing in the forest. On the left is a fountain and a great statue of Eros. In the center rear are rocks connected by a high bridge. In the distance is a dense forest. Apart from minor changes in entrances and exits, Ashton has kept closely to the original story. In the second act Orion is depicted as an Oriental prince rather than a dark hunter. He lives in a rock dwelling with palms and ferns. Sylvia lies in a curtained alcove. Two of Orion's concubines offer her gifts; then Orion orders wine, with the same consequences as in Mérante's version. At Sylvia's prayer, the wall of rock opens and reveals Eros, radiant and beautiful. In Act III there is a round temple, instead of a rectangular one, before which four trumpeters announce the festival of Bacchus. After the peasants, Ceres, Jason, Persephone, and Pluto appear, two goats frisk about; then the nine Muses enter. A small image of Bacchus and then one of Dionysus are carried on stage. Eros stands beside a veiled figure on an approaching ship; he unveils the figure before Amyntas, who happily beholds his beloved Sylvia. Eros, Amyntas, and Sylvia dance solos. Then the gods gather to see the *pas de deux* of Sylvia and Amyntas. Orion appears and rushes at the pair in a rage. Sylvia flees into the temple, and Orion attacks the temple with his fists. Diana appears and slays Orion.

The ballet technique is naturally more modern than that of the first *Sylvia*. The settings, which aim at a romantic style, are too obstructive in Act I, so that the dance is a little weighed down. Orion, with his concubines, is shown in an entirely different light than in Mérante's version. The staging is laborious. Beaumont remarks that Sylvia's new dress in Act II would have to be a gift from Orion, which he does not find logical since Sylvia wants nothing from him. The solo of Eros in the last act, the dance of the goats, the solo of Amyntas, the good ensemble of Apollo and the Muses, the effective theater in Sylvia's solo, and the splendid composition of the Amyntas-Sylvia *pas de deux* go far toward making the work acceptable even though it is a little out-of-date.

At the première the dancers were Margot Fonteyn (Sylvia), Michael Somes (Amyntas), Alexander Grant (Eros), John Hart (Orion), and Julia Farron (Diana).

Street Games

Ballet in one act. Book: Walter Gore. Choreography: Walter Gore. Music: Jacques Ibert. Scenery and costumes: Ronald Wilson. Première: November 11, 1952, at the Wimbledon Theatre, London, by the New Ballet Company.

CHARACTERS: a boy; a girl; children.

Scene: A river bank near Blackfriars Bridge, London. In the background, a wall with posters advertising a movie; on the other side of the wall, a network of cranes and derricks. On the left, a house with a window; on the right, a dark wall.

Dancers dressed like children come on stage. They pass the time playing different kinds of games. The girls draw the lines and numbers for hopscotch on the ground, but they are bothered by the boys who want to try their strength in a tug of war. Then the boys play rugby. The girls in turn begin to jump rope, and, exhausted finally, they lean against the wall to catch their breath.

An older boy enters with a girl; they have obviously just come from the movie and are still under the spell of the love story in the film. The children watch the boy as he opens the window for the girl to climb through. The boy is so occupied and in love that he does not see the rope which the children have stretched across his path. He stumbles and falls, but he can not be stopped by this bad joke. One of the girls writes something like "Mary loves Bill" on the wall; then the children dance off. The girl looks out the window of her house.

A stray ball comes over the wall. A girl picks it up and begins to play with it. A group of boys comes looking for the ball. The girl puts it on the ground and sits down with an innocent expression on her face. After looking in vain for the ball, the boys leave. The girl plays with the ball a few moments, then throws it back over the wall.

A game of tag takes place, after which the girls sit down exhausted again against the wall. The light becomes dimmer. The girl comes out of the house to play with the other girls. Their game is broken up by the noisy return of the boys, who stage a battle using wooden swords as weapons and trash can lids as shields.

Three girls enter. One pushes an old baby carriage full of discarded clothing; the second girl carries the third girl in her arms. The two older girls start to dress the youngest one; they put her in the carriage and off they go.

The young lover has somehow gotten hold of a little bouquet of flowers; on his knees he comes close to the window. He taps on the window and waits. Meanwhile, another boy has crept up behind him, and at the moment the window opens and the girl is going to take the flowers, he skillfully slips the bouquet out of the paper wrapper so that the girl gets only the wrapper. The girl takes the paper and slams it upside down on the head of the young lover. In the finale, the youth manages to get his flower back; the girls play their games one after another; the lovers are united; and everyone is happy.

❧

The subject of this ballet makes it sound deceptively simple. However, it really challenges the dancers with an extremely difficult task: that of expressing themselves with childlike movements. There is a little real structure to the work; rather there is successive activity. In the original cast were Angela Beyley, Constance Garfield, Elizabeth Christie, Margaret Kovac, Shelagh Miller, Jack Skinner, Kenneth Smith, and Nigel Burke.

The Afternoon of a Faun (II)

A pas de deux. Choreography: Jerome Robbins. Music: Claude Debussy. Scenery and Costumes: Irene Sharaff. Lighting: Jean Rosenthal. Première: May 14, 1953, at the New York City Center, by the New York City Ballet.

CHARACTERS: one female and one male dancer.

❧

Although set to the same Mallarmé-inspired Debussy composition as the 1912 Nijinsky ballet, Robbins' work has a somewhat different content. Robbins' faun is a dancer sitting in an abandoned ballet studio on a hot summer day. He looks at himself in a big mirror and is inspired to start practicing again. He does this with obvious pleasure. The mirror is dear to him, since it shows his own image, with which he is very well content. After a while a girl comes into the studio. She too discovers herself in the mirror and begins practicing. Like the boy she also finds pleasure in herself and her body. Finally the dancers discover each other in the mirror and commence a *pas de deux*. During the *pas de deux* the boy notices that he has a partner who is of flesh and blood; he steals a kiss. The girl sees the kiss in the mirror. Apparently she does not feel it, for she runs her hand slowly over her cheek to convince herself of its reality. She goes away, looking at herself carefully in the mirror. The young man, left behind, once more looks at himself again in the mirror with interest, then lies down on the floor to rest.

In contrast to the Diaghilev-Bakst-Nijinsky ballet, Robbins' work is a good reflection of Mallarmé's poem, which deals with ego, nonego, and narcissism. These are subjects of special interest in the ballet world, where dancers (male and female alike) sometimes prove to be bad partners because of excessive narcissism. The ballet was performed for the first time by Tanaquil LeClercq and Francisco Moncion and for the first time in Europe by Tanaquil LeClercq and Jacques d'Amboise.

Homage to the Queen

Coronation ballet in four tableaux and an apotheosis. Choreography: Frederick Ashton. Music: Malcolm Arnold. Scenery and costumes: Oliver Messel. Lighting: John Sullivan. Première: June, 1953, at Covent Garden, London, by the Sadler's Wells Ballet.

CHARACTERS: the queens of the Earth, Water, Fire, and Air; their respective husbands and retinues; Spirit of Fire; Queen Elizabeth I; Queen Elizabeth II.

A procession of the queens of the four elements, each accompanied by her prince consort and retinue, begins. Then follow four miniature ballets, devoted to the elements of Earth, Water, Fire, and Air. The curtain rises revealing a drop curtain the color of water, on which a small and a large tree are painted. On the branches, which suggest candelabra, are candles.

EARTH. The Queen of the Earth leaves her retinue and dances a solo, with many turns and light leaps on *pointe*. Her husband makes chiefly *tours en l'air*. There is also a *pas de six* by girls.

WATER. The Queen of the Water is surrounded by her naiads. Undulating movements by the dancers suggest the waves on the water. In the *pas de trois* (two females and one male dancer) the man does a number of *grandes pirouettes à la seconde*. The Queen's husband dances his solo, with the obligatory *tours en l'air*. The Queen herself achieves an undulating effect by her arm movements.

FIRE. Dancers wearing red, yellow, and smoke-colored costumes enter. The Queen of Fire dances a *pas de deux* with her husband and the Spirit of Fire (a male dancer). The husband does a variation based on pirouettes. The Spirit of Fire leaps dartingly into the air. Then two male and two female dancers do *pas de deux*.

AIR. The Queen of the Air (dressed in white) and her husband (dressed in gray) open the fourth tableau with a *pas de deux*. The form of the dance is acrobatic. The husband has considerably more work than usual; here he must execute a number of original and daring lifts. The dance ends as the Queen is lifted high in the air.

APOTHEOSIS. A gauze curtain comes down and then rises to disclose a figure, who obviously represents Queen Elizabeth I. She is dressed in gold brocade and stands on a flight of steps. A figure representing Queen Elizabeth II, also clothed in a dress of gold, stands a little lower. All pay homage to the monarchs.

This is a well-constructed ballet by Ashton, the only British choreographer who seems disposed to create ballets without subjects. It requires well-trained dancers and a very large stage to achieve its full effect.

The pairings of the dancers at the première were: Earth, Nadia Nerina-Alexis Rassine; Water, Violetta Elvin-John Hart; Fire, Beryl Grey-John Hart-Alexander Grant (Spirit of Fire); Air, Margot Fonteyn-Michael Somes.

Agon

Ballet in three parts. Choreography: George Balanchine. Music: Igor Stravinsky. Costumes: practice clothes. Lighting: Nananne Porcher. Première: November 27, 1957, at the New York City Center, by the New York City Ballet.

EXECUTANTS: twelve dancers: eight girls, four men.

PART I.
Pas de quatre, danced by four young men.
Double Pas de quatre, danced by eight girls.
Triple Pas de quatre, danced by eight girls and four young men.
PART II.
First *Pas de trois:* Sarabande, danced by young man A; Gaillard, danced by girls a and b; Coda, danced by young man A and girls a and b.

Second *Pas de trois:* Bransle Simple, danced by young men B and C; Bransle Gay, danced by girl c; Bransle double (de Poitot) danced by girls b and c and young men B and C.

Pas de deux, danced by young man D and girl d.
PART III.
Danse des quatre duos.
Danse des quatre trios.
Coda, danced by four young men.

Lincoln Kirstein, director of the New York City Ballet, asked Stravinsky to compose music for a composition which would be choreographed by Balanchine and executed by the New York City Ballet in honor of Stravinsky's seventy-fifth birthday. Stravinsky responded with *Agon, ballet pour douze danseures*, which he dedicated to Kirstein and Balanchine. Agon is the Greek word for contest, but here it signifies nothing more than a competition among dancers. The composition is based on dances taken from a seventeenth-century French dance manual, and Stravinsky worked on it from the end of 1953 to April, 1957. The first performance was given at Los Angeles on June 17, 1957.

Once again the Stravinsky-Balanchine combination proved very fruitful. Both artists belong in principle to the abstract school. Music, says Stravinsky, can not express anything but music. And Balanchine calls his ballet "a measured construction in space, demonstrated by moving bodies set to certain patterns or sequence in rhythm or melody with multiple ingenuities." Balanchine had already used this style for his masterwork *Four Temperaments* (1946). The première of the ballet book took place on November 27, 1957, at a benefit performance in New York; the formal première was given on December 1, 1957.

The dancers at the première were: Todd Bolender (Sarabande); Barbara Walczak and Barbara Milberg (Gaillard); Roy Tobias and Jonathan Watts (Bransle Simple); Melissa Hayden (Bransle Gay); Diana Adams and Arthur Mitchell (Pas de deux).

There have been two other versions of *Agon* which should be mentioned. One was presented on May 8, 1958, by the Hanover Opera dancers, with choreography by Yvonne Georgi. As with Balanchine, Yvonne Georgi also followed the composer's instructions as to the structure of the ballet and the number of dancers to be used; and like Balanchine, she composed an abstract work. Here is a sporting competition that avoids virtuousity and makes splendid use of the group work of dancers.

The other version was presented on August 20, 1958, at Covent Garden, by the Royal Ballet, with choreography by Kenneth MacMillan. In this production, the young choreographer MacMillan allowed himself a subject as a guideline: young people who are passing the time in a café at the edge of the city. There is, of course, a little love story involved, but the end differs from the usual "lived happily ever after" because the café proprietor and the proprietress reveal themselves to be the fate that carries off the young girl. The young man is left alone, says MacMillan, and that is life. Georgadis, who designed the scenery and costumes and has often worked with MacMillan, used clear strong colors for the scenery. The young men wore bulging blouses; the girls wore a harlequin-like costume with a short skirt that barely covered the hips.

APPENDIXES

REMARKS ON THE BALLET

An interpretation of the art of ballet,
by Dr. L. Hornstra, President of the
Circle of Dutch Dance Critics

The art of ballet is primarily an art of movement. It has taken a long time for this art to emancipate itself, and the ballets described in this book show clearly that complete emancipation is still far from achievement.

It is important not to lose ourselves exclusively in the content of the ballets and in the history of ballet art. Above all, we must take into account the essential elements: the movements. If we want to make clear what we mean by "dance movements," a comparison with music will be helpful. Let us assume that music is the highest standard of anything that can be called art; and then let us measure the art of dance against the highest standard.

There is a pretty well abandoned idea concerning music—the idea that music can communicate or depict events and situations. According to this theory, a composer would be able to depict in his compositions parts of a Spanish city, impressions at a picture exhibition, skeletons rising from their graves, or storms and rain on the plain. The titles that composers have sometimes given their works have contributed to this misunderstanding. Still more has been done in this direction by imitative sounds (onomatopoeia): bells, bird cries, thunder, wind machines, trumpet calls, the nightingale's song, the sound of the sea. The fact that these onomatopoetic and similar allusions can be put into a composition does not imply that the music always has these significations. On the contrary, these elements must fit into the musical structure, on penalty of being unmusical. Beethoven's *Pastoral Symphony* acquires its value not from any representation of country life, which it is supposed to depict,

179

but from its musical form and structure. The imitative sounds are acceptable then to the extent that they enter into this musical form.

The clearest proof of the untenability of the statement that music can depict a subject, an event, or a situation is the fact that nobody, unless he knows the subject (perhaps the title) in advance, can state even approximately what is depicted by music he has just heard. It is easy to test this (even to make a parlor game of it) by asking those present to write down what the music played depicts.

In addition to onomatopoeia, there are certain conventions in music that vary with the cultural pattern within which the music was composed. Thus, among us, it is usual for a lullaby to be written in six-eight time, and it does not matter whether there is an infant lying in a crib or a pair of lovers in a boat rocking on the water. Operas and what is called program music (not to speak of popular music) make more or less regular use of onomatopoetic allusions and illusions and of conventions. In this way, the composer is enabled to make a connection with the action, the drama, that is represented. What is of more importance is that this connection is not obtained, and can not be obtained, by musical qualities but by nonmusical elements.

In the same way that sounds are concerned with music, movements constitute the framework of dance art. As music can be connected with a subject, an action, or a drama by means of nonmusical elements, the art of dance can also be used to depict a subject, an action, or a drama. Just as musical and nonmusical elements can be distinguished in a piece of music, we must also distinguish in a ballet between dance elements and non-dance elements. Just as we generally value a piece of music more, the fewer nonmusical elements and conventions it employs, so also we can value a ballet more, the fewer non-dance elements are incorporated into it. Just as a symphony is musically superior to an opera, a pure dance ballet is superior to a narrative ballet.

It is necessary, therefore, to make a distinction between pure dance movements (comparable to sounds and motifs in music) and non-dance-art movements (comparable to onomatopoeia and other allusions in music). It is easy to state what these latter are. What the opera is in the field of music, the narrative ballet is in the realm of dance art, so that the movements which depict the action or the drama in the narrative ballet are the non-dance movements.

At this point some preliminary distinctions should be made. We must distinguish among those movements that are characterized as *actions,* those that are called *gestures,* and those that must be given the name of *dance movements.*

Actions are purposeful. Such movements need not always be consciously directed; they may be hightly automatic, as for instance walking and bicycling, but they are aimed at achieving a specific goal.

Gestures indicate relationships. They symbolize wishes, desires, expectations, hope, and despair, with respect to someone else. Gestures constitute a language by means of which one expresses oneself with reference to the existing or desired relationship with someone else. A murderous assault is not a gesture, but an act. A clenched fist is a gesture. Giving someone a cup of tea is an action; giving someone loved or admired a bouquet of flowers is a gesture. On the other hand, when the florist hands a buyer a bunch of flowers, that is an action. An action may have the nature of a gesture, but a pure gesture is always somewhat like an exclamation. An action does not "signify" anything.* A gesture, on the other hand, always has a meaning, and this is its entire value. Gestures constitute a language —the language of gestures. It is a limited language. The art of this language, pantomime, expresses merely the "here and now," never the "then or presently," and never the "over there." To this extent, ordinary language is much broader.

Dance movements differ from actions in that they are not directed toward an objective nor do they exist for the purpose of striving toward a goal. The goal of dance movements always lies within the movements themselves, which differ from gestures in that they do not express any relations or feelings and do not constitute a "language." Gestures express something outside the gestures. A gesture of despair is not the despair itself, but it communicates despair. The gesture has significance; dance movements have no significance. This is a harsh statement, but for the time being let us use the formula that dance movements are without significance, although, of course, not meaningless.

Now that we have made some provisional distinctions, let us

---

* We do, however, speak of symbolic actions—often rather incorrectly. Movements during a washing of the hands by someone who has a washing compulsion serve to wash the hands, whatever symbolic meaning is attached in addition to "becoming clean." Even if the movements themselves have a symbolic value, they appear both as action and as symbol.

return to the comparison with music. It may well be obsolete to hold that music can communicate events and situations, but it is still generally held that music (and the same is said of other arts) communicates emotions. It jars upon most people's ears to have this power denied to music. And yet, if we are able to free ourselves of prejudices, it is quite clear that music actually cannot express any feeling. We may ask directly, if you will: What feelings? Those that the composer has put "into it"? But how does that come about? After all, we only experience music through our organs of hearing, that is, by means of vibrations of the air. Then it must be that a given sequence of sounds "signifies" a given feeling; hence, it is possible to formulate a musical grammar of feelings. But such a grammar has never been prepared, nor ever can be. It is very easy to demonstrate that the feelings which A, B, and C usually have when hearing a given piece of music differ from each other as much as they do from the feelings the composer had when he was composing it. It seems to me a monstrous idea that a composer can impress all his private feelings on us by way of his music.

The conclusion to be drawn is obvious: We can have feelings aroused by hearing music, but the feelings are typical of the hearer, not of the music nor of the composer. This conclusion is supported by the fact that biographical and psychological data concerning an artist do not contribute anything to the conception or to the enjoyment of art.

Eduard Hanslick (1825–1904), the Viennese music critic who was Wagner's enemy and an admirer of Brahms, said in his main work, *Vom musikalisch Schönen,* that music never expresses or communicates anything but itself. Nothing nonmusical can ever be expressed by music. (The word "expressed" is not quite accurate; music does not express anything; it *is* only music.) And he points out that the aria "I have lost my Eurydice" from Gluck's *Orfeo* can just as well be sung to the words "I have found my Eurydice." Others have supplied any number of similar cases. "Deeply religious melodies" turn out to have been originally scurrilous soldier songs. And the same is obvious in songs in stanzas, where the same music is used over and over again for a constantly changing content.

It does not matter therefore what emotions one may feel rising within him as he hears music. The composer is not concerned with that at all; he knows only the "forms moved in sound." In his great work *The Power of Sound,* Gurney worked this position out in full. He, too, describes music as a "sequence of sounds which have no reference to anything. It does not depict extra-musical feelings and ideas at all. A composer communicates to us his own musical states and these testify to nothing but his musical perception."

Virtually all the important musicologists now hold this position of the autonomy of music: Samson in *Musique et Vie Intérieure* has formulated this anew in our time; and Lavalle sums it up succinctly: "In music what signifies and what is signified are one and the same."

In philosophical circles much larger steps have been taken beyond deciding in favor of autonomy as against heteronomy, but heteronomy (in which music is held to be the expression of events and especially of feelings, an idea the public still likes to entertain) has been soundly defeated. And it is not merely that music has no emotional vocabulary; it is equally unable to evoke a "mood." A mood is a quality of feeling, in which the original object has been lost or repressed. To say that music can not depict a mood (but does evoke moods in us—a different mood in each of us) may also seem to be a harsh statement; but there is no valid argument to contradict it.

The conclusion is plain that there is no such thing as gay, sad, or religious music. And this is so contrary to the commonly held idea that we must ask ourselves very seriously whether we have not gone off the track. But if we inquire into the origin of the qualities of feeling, they turn out to be either very individual (one person will call a composition "mournful" and another will call it "cheerful") or based on what are called conventions—conventions that vary with the period and the pattern of culture. When Schubert was asked once to play something cheerful, he answered: "There is no cheerful music." If a cheerful text is sung to what is called the "Funeral March" of Chopin, there is no mournfulness left in it.

The time has come for us to return to the art of the dance and to state by analogy that pure dance-art ballet depicts no narrative, feeling, or mood.

Music expresses only itself, and dance expresses only itself. They are not languages, and they "signify" nothing. But they are full of meaning, as every art is full of meaning. In the final analysis our love of music is based on the fact that our "ear" is sensitive to sound, and this involves setting up an entire superstructure for "evaluation" of structure, elaboration, contrast, and thematic treatment. Likewise, our love for the art of the dance is based on the fact that our "eye" is sensitive to movements of lines traced in geometric space (or "abstract space," meaning "empty" space—not a room, a hall, or a meadow, but an inhuman space filled with lines and in fact formed by these lines), and this involves also an entire superstructure of the same evaluation of structure, elaboration, and thematic treatment.

There are, however, two important differences between music and the art of the dance. In the first place, the sensitive organ is not the same. Hearing is based on a far greater receptivity than seeing. Seeing is more active. The person who sees is more mobilized; he is the master and posits himself first, absorbing, as it were, what is seen, or holding it off at a distance. The listener surrenders; he is more subject to what he hears than the looker to what he sees; he can do less sifting and must hold himself closer. It is not difficult for him to change the pattern; he must let what is heard pass over him. An object that is seen has meaning at once, but what is heard gets its full meaning only after the time needed to hear it.

Just because each visual impression forms a simultaneous whole, the person looking can take over the successive impressions and fill them out. Thus, it is possible in this way for the dancer to suggest an undulating line that fills the entire space without its being actually present. This space effect, or creation of space, by the dancer is quite new. We can still see today from films that Anna Pavlova, for instance, did not have it at all. For a choreographer like Balanchine it is a *sine qua non*.

In music, moreover, the medium consists of sound sequences, in which the source of the sound does not matter. In the art of the dance, on the other hand, the light waves are perceived on and in and by means of the source. And the source is the human body. And now how can we maintain our assertion that dance movements have no significance, that dance art is just as "abstract" as music and must be judged by the same high standard? If the art of the dance is only visible and perceptible through the human body, which is so significant, is not a purely abstract dance art a fiction? Is not the art of abstract movement reserved to such film experiments as those of Oskar Fischinger, rather than to creative choreographers and executant dancers? And is the art of ballet then not reduced to pantomime, or perhaps to Étienne Decroux's special intermediate form of "mime," in which the movements still clearly show the nature of action but are subsumed in a play of stylization, sometimes rhythmic and sometimes non-rhythmic? Is it true then that every dance movement, every "non-significant" movement, bears with it its origin in action or gesture?

The consequence of an affirmative answer to these questions would mean that in the last analysis ballet would deal with a sort of "language" of movements and hence depict dramas and moods. In other words, it would then be impossible to speak of dance movements as such. But this in turn is completely in contradiction with experience, both in the art of ballet and most folk dances.

It is obvious that dance art has its own problems, which are unknown to music. We can not try to deprive ballet art of its medium, the human body, and at the same time endeavor to maintain "abstract" (i.e., "non-significant") movement unimpaired. This implies that *dance movements proper must be wrested each time from the body, which is so human. They must be stripped of any "communicative" function and, thus abstracted, put together in compositions of movements* which make possible the same sort of aesthetic thrill as music. *The fact that this always gives rise to tensions between the body, whose tendency it is to assume significant postures, and the abstraction out of which the ballet is constructed, is precisely the distinguishing feature of ballet, in so far as it succeeds in being an art.*

And so what is really involved in ballet art is the dance movements and the composition of dance movement, not the alleged content, the subject, or the expression of all kinds of feelings. A ballet that can be described does not properly belong in the *art* of the dance.

If the most important aspect of ballet were the subject, the story, or the drama, we could only hope for a speedy death to the art of ballet. For if the guileless reader were to muster up the courage to read all the descriptions in this book, one after another, he would say to himself with a sigh that he had not realized that the *art* of ballet is so monotonous, so illogical, or unoriginal—in fact, so ridiculous. We can not put much value on the vast majority of the subjects. We take for granted all those castles and princes and bewitched princesses and moonlight and mechanical puppets. As far as its subjects are concerned, the ballet can not claim to have grown up as an art.

Things have never advanced beyond this point in Great Britain or in France. The French art of erotic display, for instance, is naturally more attractive, but if we demand more of ballet than that it soothe our own dissatisfaction, if we are really "in search of ballet art," we very soon shrug our shoulders at what are called French innovations. The young beauties are new, not the art.

Is there anything left? Enough. The Russians can teach us what true seriousness and great dedication can achieve, and what pantomime, mime acting, and staging can be. The Americans (to be sure, to some extent Russians also) teach us how enormously the art of ballet can be enriched by a freer idiom of movement. But above all we have come to realize more and more that the essence of the *art* of ballet lies in the *dance,* in dance movements, in the composition of these movements and that the art of dance is an art of space, a conquest of geometric space by melodies of movement on the basis of a musical division of time. And how is a tale about fairies or rakes concerned with that?

This book, fortunately, is directed toward what has essentially to do with the art of the dance. Does that mean that in our quest for the art of ballet we must shun most of the ballets treated in it? By no means. What we need to do is to accumulate the historical knowledge, discover true dance in the midst of nonsense, open our eyes by frequently seeing the most important ballets in history and, thus equipped, take part in the ballet culture that is being developed.

This is the idea that is expressed so clearly in this book; it is this attitude that makes this volume stand out above so many other publications on the art of the dance.

HINTS FOR THE BALLETGOER

1—A ballet should be regarded as a rhythmic-melodic play of lines formed by people (dancers) in geometric space. The choreographer is the creative artist and the dancers are merely the executants of his creation.

2—If a ballet has narrative content, do not confuse the emotional response to the story with the artistic response stimulated by the appreciation of the dance art.

3—A narrative ballet must be comprehensible in itself, without explanatory program notes.

4—The music serves principally for rhythm and measure, to divide "time" so that "space" can be more easily conquered. It is used with, or in contrast to, the rhythm and measure (and "melody") of the dance. But do not confuse the musical emotion with the ballet emotion. A good test is to look at the ballet with your ears stopped up.

5—Above all . . . look at the steps! The names are unimportant. It is better to experience a lovely arabesque or a fine attitude than to know what it is called.

6—Close your mind's eye to the settings, to the lighting, and especially to the costumes, so that nothing remains but the dancers in practice clothes. The names of the dancers are for the moment unimportant; equally unimportant is the charm of the ballerina or the handsome body or fascinating smile of a male dancer. Now, look closely at the dance, the movements, the lines, the rhythm, the "melody," the theme.

7—Only when you have learned to find the art of the dance in ballet, to appreciate it for yourself, to make distinctions, and to form judgments will you be ready to use all your other artistic senses and to permit the entire performance, as theater, affect you: story, mood, music, settings, costumes, and lighting.

8—Do not be afraid to say that something is beautiful or ugly—regardless of the opinion of your companions or your newspaper and regardless of what you thought the last time. But keep in mind that the emotion of beauty is something different from our ordinary feelings and emotions.

9—Attend many ballet performances. We learn ballet by seeing and by having experienced many performances from which we can make distinctions.

INDEX

INDEX

191